WARWICKSHIRE EDUCATION COMMITTEE

TO OPEN cut label instead of tearing envelope

A SKETCH-MAP HISTORY
OF BRITAIN

The Sketch-map Histories

General Editor: GEORGE TAYLOR, M.A.

Crown 4to

A SKETCH-MAP HISTORY
OF BRITAIN
1783—1914

BY

IRENE RICHARDS B.A.

FORMERLY HEAD OF THE HISTORY DEPARTMENT
LATYMER SCHOOL EDMONTON LONDON

AND

J. A. MORRIS B.Sc.(Econ.)

HEAD OF THE GEOGRAPHY DEPARTMENT
LATYMER SCHOOL EDMONTON LONDON

GEORGE G. HARRAP AND COMPANY LTD
LONDON   TORONTO   WELLINGTON   SYDNEY

First published in Great Britain **1937**
by GEORGE G. HARRAP & CO. LTD
*182 High Holborn, London, W.C.*1

Reprinted: August 1938; *April* 1939; *January* 1940; *June* 1941;
October 1942; *October* 1944; *September* 1945; *July* 1946;
January 1948; *April* 1949; *January* 1953; *May* 1954;
December 1955; *May* 1957; *October* 1959; *July* 1960;
December 1961, *September* 1963

Made in Great Britain. Printed by Morrison & Gibb, Ltd.
London and Edinburgh

PREFACE

THIS book follows closely the line set by Mr Taylor's companion volume on modern European history. It is similarly addressed mainly to senior pupils of secondary schools who are preparing for examinations, more especially for the General Certificate of Education (Ordinary Level).

The authors are convinced that students benefit greatly from sketch-map studies and especially from maps they have drawn themselves. The examples in this book are intended merely as suggestions, and pupils should be encouraged to redraw them. building up the sketch-map from an outline map as the historical material is assimilated, Our experience goes to show that in this way not only is the work of memorizing simplified, but the inter-relations of diverse facts are more vividly grasped.

The authors have had no intention to stress unduly the geographical factors in historical development, but where a more detailed geographical analysis seemed desirable (*e.g.*, Maps 1 and 31) it has been included.

The great indebtedness of the authors for material and ideas collected from many diverse sources is gladly acknowledged. To the general editor thanks are given for permission to use and remodel Maps 4, 14, 19, 32 and for general advice and encouragement generously given at all stages of the work. The help of our colleagues is appreciated, in particular that of Mr J. B. Goodson, M.A., for many hints and the special note on p. 9. The helpful criticism of friends has led to improvements in all sections of the work. Further suggestions for making this sketch-map history more useful will be gratefully received.

IRENE RICHARDS
J. A. MORRIS

LATYMER SCHOOL
EDMONTON, N.9

5

CONTENTS

INTRODUCTION

EVERY history-student knows the temptation to pass over the numerous place-names that occur in his reading without discovering their locations or asking himself what significance is to be attached to them. He knows that if he neglects the necessary references to atlases and maps his historical knowledge is in danger of becoming a vague acquaintance with happenings 'far away and long ago.' When, however, the scene of historical action is clearly visualized, certainty and confidence are gained. Moreover, it frequently happens that the mere knowledge of where certain historical events occurred explains their importance. The complete understanding which then results makes it impossible to forget the facts.

Examine, for example, the map illustrating the critical year of 1797 (p. 20) and the battles of Camperdown and Cape St Vincent. These battles were once described by a casual pupil as " two sea-fights that we won (I think) somewhere or other—I forget when ! " Such incomplete and worthless information suggests that he had never understood the purpose of these engagements. Had he drawn a map showing the plan of a triple attack, he would have realized the danger averted by the successful tackling of the ' wing three-quarters.' Then the facts would have become really memorable.

Even where the location of a place appears to have little significance it is poor scholarship to be able to recite, for example, that John Wesley was born at Epworth and to have no idea where the place is. It pretends to a knowledge which does not exist.

The historical and the physical atlases should, of course, be used for such purposes, and this book does not claim to replace them. What it does do is to supply simple maps which show only those facts that are likely to be required when a particular topic is being studied. Thus the effort of searching for place-names is reduced, and the omission of detail irrelevant to the topic simplifies both the map and the pupil's task. The plethora of information in many historical atlases is overwhelming to the young mind, and it is hoped that the simplification of these maps will make the pupil more prone to use maps regularly during his history-reading.

This book is not intended as a mere reference work, however. Many of its maps go much farther; they actually ' tell the story ' and will repay very careful study. Experiment has shown that a very good account of the Waterloo Campaign, for example, can be written using no data beyond that shown on Map 4.

The notes are intended to link the facts shown on the maps with the general historical background. The student should continually refer from notes to map, and when the former are well known he should study the map itself closely and critically.

He should realize, however, that reading and looking are not enough in themselves. Maps must be *drawn* if they are to be remembered. Elaborate copies should not be made. Simple sketches illustrating a few points only should be preferred. The sketch-map for 1797 referred to above provides an example of how to select from the larger map just those points which bear on a single problem.

Especial care must be taken if an attempt is made to represent on one map events of two different periods. The general appearance of sketch-maps will be improved by (a) enclosing the sketch in a box, (b) avoiding Chinese printing, *i.e.*, $\frac{\text{C}}{\text{H}}_\text{I}_\text{N}_\text{A}$, (c) making the map a reasonable size, and (d) using arrows to indicate movement.

The use of a few bold colours will simplify the task and increase the satisfaction obtained from a piece of work well done.

J. B. G.

GREAT BRITAIN IN THE WORLD OF 1783

Up to the sixteenth century the British Isles lay on the fringe of the known world, which centred round the Mediterranean Sea. The discovery of the New World revolutionized the importance of the countries on the Atlantic seaboard ; they began to enjoy the trading advantages of the most favourable geographical position. Most fortunate of all these West European countries was Britain, whose superiority in industry and commerce was becoming increasingly marked.

The advantages enjoyed by the British Isles were :

A. Natural

(1) *Islands*. The insular character gave security. There was no devastation of the English countryside by warfare such as harassed the development of the continental countries. No foreign armies have landed in Great Britain since the Middle Ages.

(2) Moreover, the *shape* and *structure* of the islands increased the advantages due to position :

(a) The indented coast provided excellent harbours and brought all parts of the interior within easy access of sea-water.

(b) Though by no means a uniform level plain, the relief of the islands was not sufficiently marked to embarrass movement between the different parts of the country. Neither mountain barrier nor impassable marsh prevented the building of roads (or, later, railways). Canal-construction, sometimes difficult, was not impossible.

(c) The mineral wealth provided the raw materials necessary for the development of manufacturing-industries ; coal and iron were found in close proximity to each other and to the sea.

(3) *Climate*. The temperate climate was a further stimulus to progress. Extremes of enervating heat or repellent cold were alike unknown. The seasonal diversity nurtured an energetic race. Rivers and ports were never ice-bound. Excessive snow-falls rarely hampered communications. The humid climate favoured the textile industries.

B. Political and Social

(4) *Economic advantages of the Empire*. The colonial possessions of Britain were valuable (a) as a source of raw materials and food which could not be grown in temperate latitudes, and (b) as a secure market for the sale of manufactured goods. The extension of colonial territory had three important results on British industry :

(a) the volume of trade was increased ;

(b) inventions to increase production to meet the enlarged demand were stimulated ;

(c) the increased demand for manufactured goods made it possible to introduce methods of large-scale production.

(5) *Command of the Sea*. The predominant position of British shipping in the commerce of the world and the power of the Navy to protect it gave Britain the means of carrying her goods safely all over the world.

MAP I

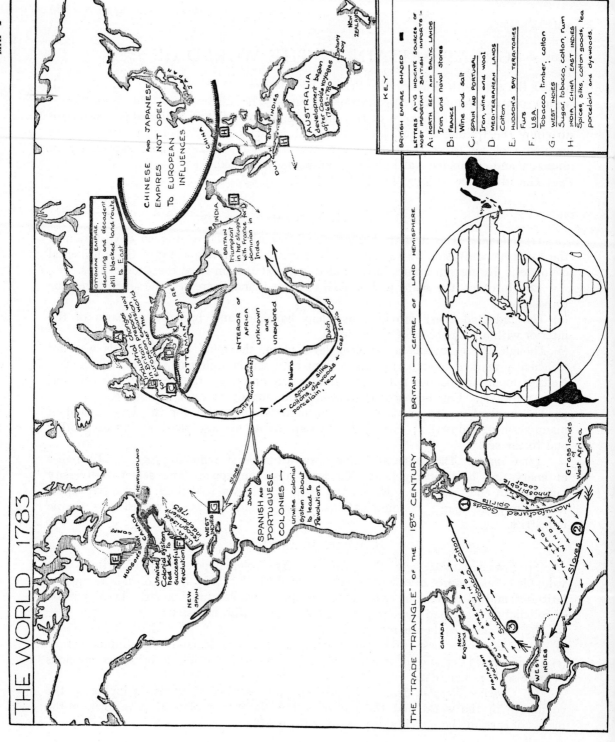

THE WORLD 1783

CHINESE and JAPANESE EMPIRES NOT OPEN To EUROPEAN INFLUENCES

OTTOMAN EMPIRE, declining and decadent still blocked land route to East.

BRITAIN Triumphant in her struggle with France for Dominion in India.

Industrial change was the prime reason Britain prospered as the European power of the world.

INTERIOR of AFRICA Unknown and Unexplored

AUSTRALIA development began after Cook's voyages 1768-1780

St Helena

Forts along Coast

Spices, cottons, silks, dyewoods, porcelain, tea.

East India Co.

Dutch Co.

Slaves

SPANISH and PORTUGUESE COLONIES

Unwise colonial system about to lead to Revolution.

WEST INDIES

NEW SPAIN

NEWFOUNDLAND

HUDSON'S BAY CANADA COMPY

Unwise Colonial system had led to successful War of Independence 1783

New ZEALAND Botany Bay

CHINA

INDIA

DUTCH EAST INDIES

OTTOMAN EMPIRE

THE "TRADE TRIANGLE" OF THE 18TH CENTURY

BRITAIN — CENTRE OF LAND HEMISPHERE.

Manufactured Goods

Slaves

Cotton

TOBACCO, COTTON & SUGAR

Grasslands of West Africa

Inhospitable coastline

CANADA

New England

Plantation States

WEST INDIES

KEY

BRITISH EMPIRE SHADED

LETTERS A–G INDICATE SOURCES of MOST IMPORTANT BRITISH IMPORTS:-

A: NORTH SEA AND BALTIC LANDS
Iron and naval stores

B: FRANCE
Wine and salt

C: SPAIN AND PORTUGAL
Iron, wine and wool

D: MEDITERRANEAN LANDS
Cotton

E: HUDSON'S BAY TERRITORIES
Furs

F: USA
Tobacco, timber, cotton

G: WEST INDIES
Sugar, tobacco, cotton, rum

H: INDIA, CHINA, EAST INDIES
Spices, silks, cotton goods, tea, porcelain and dyewoods.

(6) In the nineteenth century, possible continental rivals were more concerned with wars and internal revolt than with economic progress. While European nations struggled for democracy or fought for freedom, Britain remained neutral, sold them arms, clothes, and other manufactures, captured their trade, and carried their goods. The political struggles in the seventeenth century had given Britain a stable constitutional Government which could keep order and secure the legal rights and property of the British people.

(7) There was in England a comparative absence of the social barriers—class and caste distinctions—which divided the peoples of Europe and the East. It was possible for a yeoman farmer or a barber's assistant to become a cotton king. The English aristocracy were not averse to making profit in trade and industry (*cf.* the Duke of Bridgewater and canal-construction).

People were free to move about and work where they wished to a degree unknown on the Continent, where feudal restrictions still fettered the people.

C. ECONOMIC

(8) Internal barriers to trade had long been swept away, and the medieval gild, with its conservative restrictions, no longer exercised any control over industrial development.

(9) *Labour.* The enclosure movement caused dispossessed agricultural workers from the countryside to find employment in the towns (p. 71). They provided a supply of cheap labour to work the new machines. In other countries, where the peasantry remained on the land, there was difficulty in attracting labour to the factories (*cf.* modern Japan).

(10) *Capital.* The accumulated profits derived from trade and commerce in the seventeenth and eighteenth centuries provided capital to finance the changes in industry and agriculture.

THE DECLINE OF THE OLD COLONIAL EMPIRES

For three centuries after the discovery of the Americas there had been competition among the nations of Western Europe for sea-power and colonial wealth. Britain had struggled successively against Spain, Holland, and France. By 1783, when the period of competition came to an end, she was supreme on the seas and on the point of becoming the leading colonial and commercial nation in the world.

The colonial powers were Portugal, Spain, France, Holland, and England. They all regarded colonies as spheres of trade monopoly, useful sources of tropical products, of precious metals, distant places to be exploited for the benefit of the mother countries. This attitude led at first to friction, and later to revolution. The American colonies of England had declared their independence; the Spanish and Portuguese colonies were ripe for revolt.

Spain. England had struggled against Spain in the sixteenth century for the right to share in the trade of the New World. In the eighteenth century Spain still held vast possessions in America, but the Spanish Government was fast losing its hold. Colonists and foreigners alike combined to break down the commercial monopoly and exclusiveness imposed upon them.

Portugal. From the seventeenth century Dutch and English merchants shared with Portugal the rich trade of the East. In the West the prosperous colony of Brazil was beginning to resent the restrictive regulations of the Lisbon Government. The desire for freedom was growing.

Holland. The Dutch had declined relatively since the seventeenth century. They had lost their lucrative carrying-trade and, though still possessing the East Indies, they were no longer serious rivals in any other part of the world.

France. The eighteenth century had witnessed a struggle between France and England in India and Canada ; in both countries Britain emerged triumphant.

THE NEW BRITISH EMPIRE

The foundations of a new empire were already laid in 1783.

(*a*) *North America.* The loss of the American colonies was a great blow, but Canada had remained loyal, and Britain still retained an important foothold on the North American Continent. After the war of 1783 the United Empire Loyalists left the revolting states and set up new homes on the shores of the great lakes and along the St Lawrence valley. Canada was thus developed, and British power there was strengthened (see Map 26).

(*b*) *India.* The defeat of the French had made Britain predominant. No rival colonial power hampered the gradual extension of the territory of the East India Company from its bases in Bengal, Madras, and Bombay (see Map 29).

(*c*) *Australia.* Captain Cook's scientific expeditions (1769–1774) had opened up a new field of activity for British enterprise in Australia and New Zealand.

(*d*) *Africa.* A few coastal settlements which were important because of the slave-trade were the only British possessions in Africa. Nevertheless it was from these sea-board holdings that Britain penetrated into the interior of the Continent. (*N.B.* The vast British territories to-day are largely explained by the fact that by 1783 Britain had won the right to coastal strips in Africa, India, and Australia.)

(*e*) *West Indies.* Certain islands in the West Indies were the most cherished of all British possessions, and in the days when Britain was self-sufficing as regards wheat and meat (*i.e.*, food-necessities) the sugar, cotton, rum, tobacco, and mahogany (*i.e.*, luxuries) brought from the Indies were the staple commodities of overseas trade.

PRE-EMINENCE OF GREAT BRITAIN

The map shows that in 1783 there was scarcely a continent which did not provide Britain with unrivalled openings for development. For almost a hundred years no foreign rival became formidable, and British traders and manufacturers were able to take advantage of their unique opportunities.

BRITAIN IN 1783

THE preceding map shows the position of Great Britain in relation to the rest of the world. This map attempts to give a picture of the general conditions within the country.

ENGLAND

A. SOCIETY

England was an aristocratic country. Vast changes were taking place at this time, but eighty per cent. of the people still lived as they had done for centuries in the country; their lives were centred in the village and their loyalties in the local squires. As yet the relations between the gentry and the people continued to be friendly, and there was little social unrest; but agricultural changes were soon to destroy the old order.

This was a happy age for the aristocracy. They had great privileges, and they used their influence to promote the welfare of their rural communities. At the same time they were actively interested in art, literature, and politics; they set themselves high standards of taste and duty.

B. ECONOMIC CONDITIONS

(1) *Agriculture.* A steady increase in population from the beginning of the eighteenth century, with an increased demand for food, stimulated the introduction of new methods for improving farming. These new methods led to the disappearance, through enclosure, of the open fields and common pastures where they still existed— *i.e.*, in the Midland counties. (For description of Agrarian Revolution, see Map 20 and notes on pp. 71–73.)

(2) *Trade.* During the eighteenth century there was an enormous expansion of overseas trade (see preceding map and notes), and the construction of roads and canals (Maps 21 and 22 and pp. 75–77) stimulated the movement of goods within the country.

The profits gained in the increased volume of trade provided an abundance of commercial capital, while the developing banking-system provided increased facilities for borrowing money to use in industry and trade.

The growth of the power and influence of great trading-companies—especially the East India Company—and the rapid rise of the port of Liverpool reflect the extent of this commercial expansion.

(3) *Industry.* In 1783 the changes that were to make England the workshop of the world were already beginning.

(a) *The woollen industry,* the predominant English industry for the past three hundred years, was still carried on in the home, but most of the workers had ceased to be masters and had become wage-earners.

(b) *New industries,* founded from the sixteenth century onward, were still on a small scale but were ready for great expansion (*e.g.*, the cotton-industry and iron- and steel-making with coal).

(c) *Inventions* called into being by the scarcity of labour were eagerly accepted by manufacturers.

MAP 2

BRITAIN IN 1783

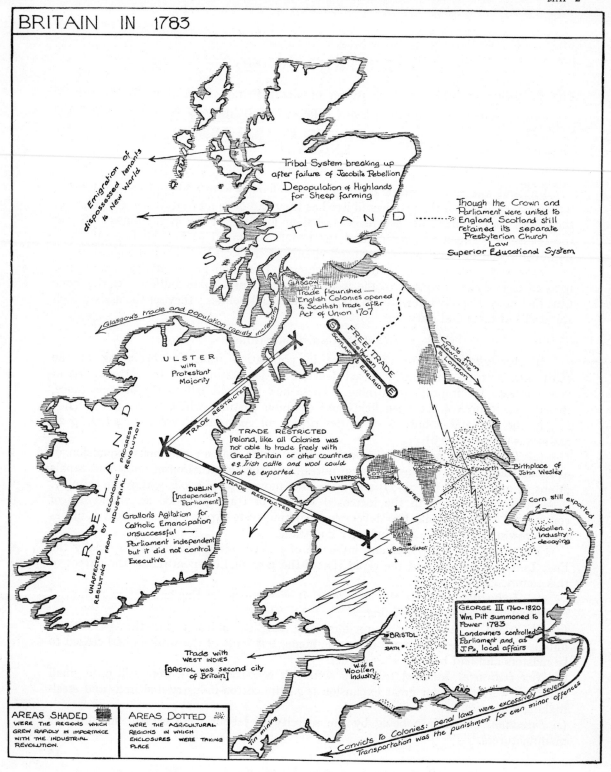

Emigration of dispossessed tenants to New World

Tribal System breaking up after failure of Jacobite Rebellion

Depopulation of Highlands for Sheep farming

SCOTLAND

Though the Crown and Parliament were united to England, Scotland still retained its separate
Presbyterian Church
Law
Superior Educational System

GLASGOW
Trade flourished — English Colonies opened to Scottish trade after Act of Union 1707

Glasgow's trade and population rapidly increasing

ULSTER with Protestant Majority

FREE TRADE between Scotland and England

Coals from Newcastle & London

TRADE RESTRICTED

TRADE RESTRICTED
Ireland, like all Colonies was not able to trade freely with Great Britain or other countries e.g. Irish cattle and wool could not be exported.

LIVERPOOL

COTTON

MANCHESTER

Epworth

Birthplace of John Wesley

IRELAND unaffected by economic progress resulting from Industrial Revolution

DUBLIN [Independent Parliament]

TRADE RESTRICTED

Grattan's Agitation for Catholic Emancipation unsuccessful — Parliament independent but it did not control Executive

WOOLLENS

METALS

BIRMINGHAM

Corn still exported

Woollen industry decaying

GEORGE III 1760-1820
Wm. Pitt summoned to Power 1783
Landowners controlled Parliament and, as J.Ps, local affairs

BRISTOL
BATH

Trade with WEST INDIES
[Bristol was second city of Britain]

W. of E. Woollen Industry

Convicts to Colonies: penal laws were excessively severe. Transportation was the punishment for even minor offences

Tin mining

AREAS SHADED ▓ WERE THE REGIONS WHICH GREW RAPIDLY IN IMPORTANCE WITH THE INDUSTRIAL REVOLUTION.

AREAS DOTTED ⠦ WERE THE AGRICULTURAL REGIONS IN WHICH ENCLOSURES WERE TAKING PLACE (*d*) *The natural resources of the country*—coal, iron, climate, position—and the wealth which was being created out of the profits of trade (see Note 2), enabled Britain to take the lead in the Industrial Revolution.

C. RELIGION

The eighteenth century had seen a great decline of religious enthusiasm after the intense absorption in religion shown in the sixteenth and seventeenth centuries. The Church of England was rich in goods, but spiritually poor ; the parish priests had become subservient to the squire. In the rapidly growing towns religious influences rarely reached the industrial workers.

These conditions were transformed by :

(1) *John Wesley*. Devoting himself to bringing the Gospel to the working-classes, he changed the spiritual lives of thousands of miners and workers in the coalfields of the North, the Midlands, and South Wales. Disdained by the Church of England, his followers founded the Methodist Church.

(2) The *Evangelicals*. A group of the Anglican clergy inspired by Wesley's work, the Evangelicals, brought a new spirit into the Church itself. They set out to improve social conditions.

(*a*) Prison-reform was advocated by John Howard (1726–1790).

(*b*) The slave-trade was attacked by Wilberforce and Clarkson.

(*c*) Sunday Schools were founded by Robert Raikes to enable the children of the town-workers to read the Bible.

D. GOVERNMENT

The Revolution of 1688 had made Parliament supreme over the King, and had given the Whig landlords control over Parliament as well as over local government. They maintained their influence by means of the corrupt system of parliamentary representation and the still greater corruption in the municipal government of the cities and towns. The attempts of George III to exploit corruption to dominate the House of Commons first led to demands for reform. Reform was supported in many quarters until the outbreak of the French Revolution, which caused the governing classes to resist all change.

SCOTLAND

Many striking changes had taken place since the beginning of the century following the Union with England in 1707 and the two Jacobite rebellions.

(*a*) The former had led to the economic development of the lowlands ; the Scottish merchants obtained free trade with the colonies, and Glasgow became a great port. The new agricultural methods were introduced (see Map 20).

(*b*) The rebellions led to the break-up of the clans. The Highland chiefs introduced sheep-farming and evicted the clansmen no longer useful to them for their fighting power. The glens became depopulated.

Parish schools set up by the Presbyterian Kirk flourished, and the mass of the people enjoyed a much higher standard of culture than in England.

B

IRELAND

The condition of Ireland was very different. There had been no progress for the following reasons :

(*a*) the landlords were different in race and religion from the people. Living in England, they were concerned only with the rents they obtained from their Irish lands.

(*b*) *Land-hunger*. Ireland was over-populated. The introduction of the potato in the eighteenth century provided a cheap and easily grown food, and the population grew rapidly at a rate hitherto unknown in Western Europe. In 1741 it was less than 2,000,000 ; in 1841 it was over 8,000,000. Most of these people lived on the verge of starvation. The demand for land reduced the holdings to sizes incompatible with proper cultivation, and the competition for land raised the rent beyond the amount that the soil could return in produce. (Refer also to Map 18 and notes pp. 63–66.)

(*c*) Penal laws had restricted progress by preventing Catholic education and purchase of land.

(*d*) Trade-restrictions had been imposed by the British Government in the interests of farmers and manufacturers in Great Britain.

The Irish Parliament had just gained its independence (1782), but it represented only Protestants, and was not a fit instrument to alleviate the misery of Ireland. Some progress was, however, made ; restrictions on Irish exports were removed in 1780. In 1785 Pitt tried in vain to establish complete free trade between Ireland and Great Britain ; this was achieved by the Act of Union in 1801.

PITT'S FOREIGN POLICY (1783-1793)

PITT became Prime Minister at a time when the disaster of the American War of Independence had created great problems at home. At first he was not greatly interested in foreign affairs, his main object being to improve the financial stability of the country. The maintenance of peace and the security of the British Isles were the motives of his increasing interest in foreign policy.

The main threat to peace in the mind of an eighteenth-century statesman was a disturbance of the balance of power by any one of the great states. In the years 1783-1789 the balance was threatened by the ambitions of France in the West and Russia in the East.

(1) *France.* France was eager to acquire influence in Holland and the Austrian Netherlands; control of this region would have facilitated interference with English shipping and the invasion of England, as well as putting the important ports of Antwerp and Rotterdam—rivals to London—in French hands.

(a) *Holland.* The French assisted the revolutionary activities of the patriots who were trying to overthrow William of Orange. To meet this danger Pitt made an agreement with Prussia and Holland (the Triple Alliance of 1788). Common action by the alliance restored the Prince and ended the intrigues of the French.

(b) *The Austrian Netherlands.* These were in revolt against Joseph II of Austria, who was trying to establish uniformity in the government of the Hapsburg dominions. France was intriguing with the democratic parties in the Netherlands. Pitt held that action to prevent the union of the Austrian lands with France was worth the risk of war, and he assured the Belgians that Britain would not allow the Emperor to crush them. His diplomacy weakened the influence of France. As will appear, the invasion of the Netherlands by the French Republican Army in 1792 forced Pitt to war.

(c) *Trade treaty of 1786.* To create better relations with France Pitt negotiated a free-trade treaty in 1786. It did not improve political relations, but it did benefit the trade of both countries until the Revolution broke out.

(2) *Russia.* During the eighteenth century Russia's expansion had been enormous, and Pitt was alarmed. Catharine II, wishing to control the entrance to the Mediterranean, determined on the partition of the decaying Turkish Empire. In opposing Russia and supporting Turkey Pitt laid down a cardinal principle of British foreign policy for the next century. Despite his protests Catharine acquired a fortified port, Otchakoff, thus taking a step towards Constantinople.

(3) *The Pacific Coast of North America.* A small incident in 1790 had a far-reaching effect. The Spanish Government seized some British ships at Nootka Sound, near Vancouver Island, and claimed the whole Pacific coast for Spain. By strong action Pitt compelled Spain to yield; so the western coast was kept free for the needs of U.S.A. and Canada in the future.

MAP 3

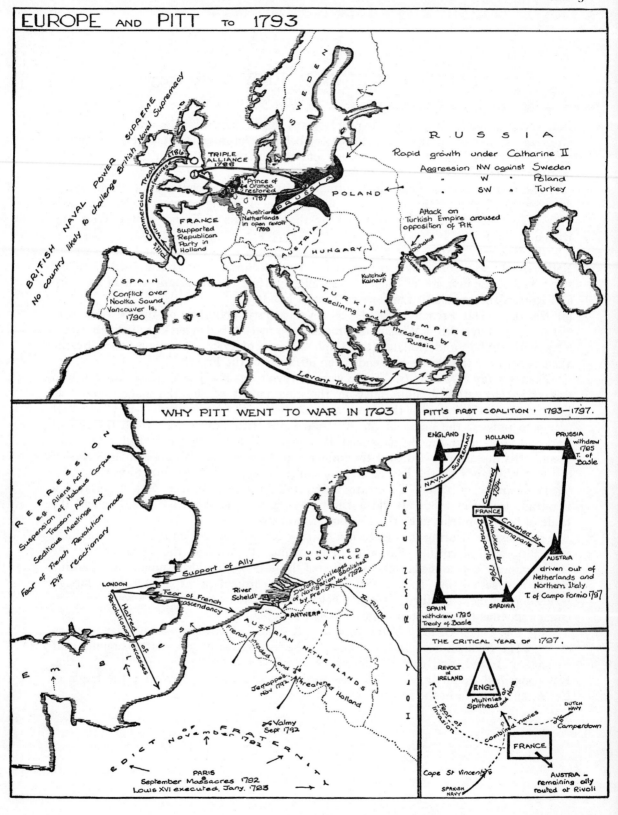

WHY ENGLAND AND FRANCE WENT TO WAR IN 1793

The map shows the circumstances that destroyed Pitt's hope of keeping England at peace.

(1) *French attack on the Netherlands and Savoy.* Austria and Prussia had declared war on France in 1792. After the defeat of the Prussian army at Valmy in 1792, the French overran the Netherlands, over which they gained control by their victory over the Austrians at Jemappes.

(2) *Defiance of treaty regulations.* Antwerp fell, and the French declared the port and its river, the Scheldt, open to the trade of the world. The Treaty of Utrecht, of 1713, had included a provision—imposed in the interests of Great Britain—that navigation of the Scheldt was to be confined to Dutch and British shipping.

(3) *Threat to invade Holland.* Though Holland had remained neutral there was a danger of its invasion by the French.

(4) *The ' Edict of Fraternity.'* A decree of the Revolutionary Government in 1792 called on all the nations to overthrow their rulers and to set up republics. Pitt and the governing classes feared that French propaganda would provoke a revolution in England.

(5) *Revolutionary excesses in France.* The September Massacres of defenceless men and women in Paris had aroused an outcry in England. The extreme party, the Jacobins, gained increasing influence and secured the execution of Louis XVI in 1793. Public opinion in England was horrified and clamoured for war.

N.B. France declared war on England in 1793.

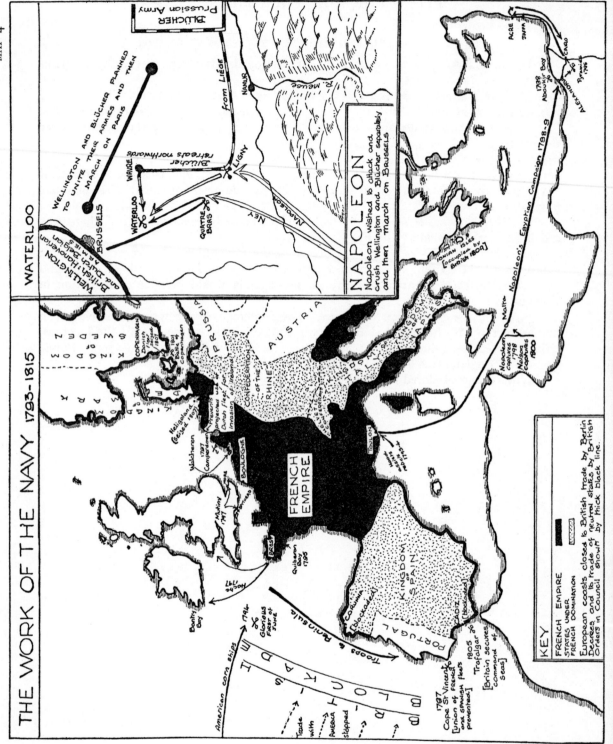

MAP 4

THE WORK OF THE NAVY 1793-1815

WATERLOO

BLÜCHER Prussian Army

WELLINGTON AND BLÜCHER PLANNED TO UNITE THEIR ARMIES AND THEN MARCH ON PARIS

BRUSSELS

WELLINGTON British; Hanoverian and Dutch-Belgian Armies

WATERLOO

WAVRE

QUATRE BRAS

LIGNY

Blücher retreats northwards

NEY

NAPOLEON

from Liége

NAMUR

R. MEUSE

NAPOLEON

Napoleon wished to attack and crush Wellington and Blücher separately and then march on BRUSSELS

KINGDOM of SWEDEN

KINGDOM of DENMARK

COPENHAGEN Danish fleet seized 1807 Battle of Copenhagen 1801

Heligoland (seized 1807)

Walcheren 1809 Campaign projected use of Dutch Fleet prevents invasion of Ireland

PRUSSIA

CONFEDERATION OF THE RHINE

AUSTRIA

HELVETIC REPUBLIC

KINGDOM of ITALY

KINGDOM of NAPLES

IONIAN ISLES [occupied by British 1809]

Malta

Napoleon captures 1798 Nelson recaptures 1800

ACRE 1799

Aboukir Bay 1798

ALEXANDRIA 1798 Napoleon's Egyptian Campaign 1798-9

ABOUKIR Pyramids 1798 CAIRO 1798

FRENCH EMPIRE

BOULOGNE

TOULON

Mutiny 1797

Bantry Bay

PARIS

Quiberon Bay 1795

Hoche 1797

American corn ships 1794

B L O C K A D E

Glorious First of June

1797 Cape St Vincent [Union of French and Spanish fleets prevented]

Troops & Peninsula

CORUNNA [Blockaded]

CADIZ [blocked]

1805 Trafalgar [Britain secures command of seas]

KINGDOM of PORTUGAL

KINGDOM of SPAIN

Trade with AMERICA stopped

KEY

FRENCH EMPIRE

STATES UNDER FRENCH DOMINATION

European coasts closed to British trade by Berlin Decrees and its trade of neutral states by British Orders in Council shown by thick black line.

THE WORK OF THE BRITISH NAVY (1793–1815)

THE map illustrates the important work of the Navy during the French Wars.

A. DEFENCE OF OUR SHORES

(1) At the beginning of the Revolutionary Wars (1793–1802) the Navy was un-prepared, and no bolder policy was adopted than that of defending our shores from invasion and the protection of British shipping. Two engagements took place in the opening year of the war :

(a) The help given by the British fleet to the rebels at Toulon in 1793.

(b) Admiral Lord Howe's victory in 1794—the ' Glorious First of June.'

Both engagements failed in their purpose ; the English were driven from Toulon by Napoleon, and the corn-ships which Howe tried to intercept reached France in safety.

(2) *The dangerous year of 1797 : control of the Channel.* The Directory planned a triple attack on the British Isles by the allied fleets of France, Spain, and Holland.

Admiral Jervis prevented a Spanish squadron, sailing from the Mediterranean, from joining the French by his victory off Cape St Vincent. The Spanish fleet was forced to shelter in Cadiz.

Admiral Duncan held the Dutch fleet at bay at Camperdown. It was a remarkable feat, for the mutinies at the Nore and Spithead had disorganized our fleet. (Refer also to Map 3.)

These two victories once more established British supremacy in the Channel.

(3) *Battle of the Nile* (1798) *: control of the Mediterranean.* Napoleon, having persuaded the Directory to accept his plan to invade Egypt, sailed from Toulon to Alexandria, attacking Malta on his way. The French fleet anchored in Aboukir Bay.

Nelson sailed in pursuit and completely destroyed the French fleet in the Battle of the Nile.

Britain never afterwards lost control of the Mediterranean. She captured Malta, which became an important naval base.

(4) *Battle of Copenhagen* (1801) *: control of the Baltic.* One of Nelson's great achievements was his successful attack on Copenhagen and the destruction of the Danish fleet. The northern nations had formed a league to protect their commerce, and this was a serious threat to British interests in the Baltic. The ' Battle of the Baltic ' broke up the ' armed neutrality ' and enabled Britain to secure access to necessary war-materials—viz., naval stores from the Baltic lands.

B. BLOCKADE OF THE COASTS OF EUROPE

During the Napoleonic Wars (1803–1805) the British fleet blockaded the French fleets stationed in various ports and prevented their combination. This was a difficult task and occupied the attention of the greater part of the Navy, for Brest and Toulon, the two chief naval bases of the French, were far apart, and the Spanish squadrons also had to be watched.

(1) *Battle of Trafalgar* (1805) : *undisputed control of the seas.* Napoleon had determined upon the invasion of England. His army was stationed at Boulogne in 1803–1805, waiting to be escorted across the Channel by the combined French and Spanish fleets when the British blockade could be evaded. The French fleets sailed to the West Indies, Nelson in pursuit. They slipped back to join the Spanish fleet at Cadiz and were again blockaded until Admiral Villeneuve was forced by Napoleon to attack. A naval engagement was fought off Cape Trafalgar. It was the most important naval battle of the war because :

(*a*) the decisive defeat of the French navy gave Britain undisputed command of the seas ;

(*b*) there was no further danger of the invasion of Britain.

(2) *The 'Continental System.'* Napoleon's next plan was to destroy Britain's commerce by prohibiting trade with the Continent. In this economic struggle the Navy played an important part. It blockaded the coasts of Europe (shown on the map by thick lines) and occupied numerous islands from which goods could be smuggled into Europe—*e.g.*, Sicily, the Ionian Islands, and Heligoland.

(*a*) In 1807 Copenhagen was bombarded and the Danish fleet seized to frustrate Napoleon's plans.

(*b*) A further result of the trade warfare was friction between Britain and America. In the War of 1812–1814 the American navy was too weak to stop a blockade of her coasts. A number of minor engagements took place, the most famous of which was the duel between H.M.S. *Shannon* and the *Chesapeake.*

C. Attacks on Colonial Rivals

The colonies of France and her allies were attacked and seized (refer to Map 6 and notes on pp. 29–30).

D. Co-operation in Military Expeditions

It was the policy of Britain to encourage resistance to Napoleon. The Navy transported troops to the Continent and supported military operations, *e.g.*, the Walcheren Expedition (1809) and the Peninsular War (1808–1814).

E. Safeguarding Trade-routes

The French and their allies attacked British merchantmen with considerable success. One of the most important services of the Navy was to protect British shipping. French commerce was almost entirely destroyed before the end of the wars.

THE WATERLOO CAMPAIGN

While the Powers, in Congress at Vienna, were settling the affairs of Europe, news suddenly reached them that Napoleon had again become master of France. The Allies (Prussia, Austria, Russia, and England) renewed their pact to support one another until Napoleon was driven out again.

Napoleon determined upon a swift attack in Belgium before the Allies could break through his long frontier. The British and Prussians, under Wellington and Blücher, had gathered forces on the Belgian plain. Napoleon decided to act before the Russians and Austrians could send assistance.

Map 4 (inset) shows the principal features of the decisive campaign.

Results of Napoleon's defeat

(1) Napoleon's long and ambitious career came to an end. He was forced to abdicate and was exiled for life to the lonely island of St Helena.

(2) A new peace was imposed on France; Louis XVIII was restored, and, as a punishment for welcoming back Napoleon, the boundaries of France were slightly reduced. She had also to submit to an army of occupation.

(3) The British army gained immense prestige. Wellington's soldiers had proved to be a match for Napoleon's veterans.

MAP 5

THE PENINSULAR WAR

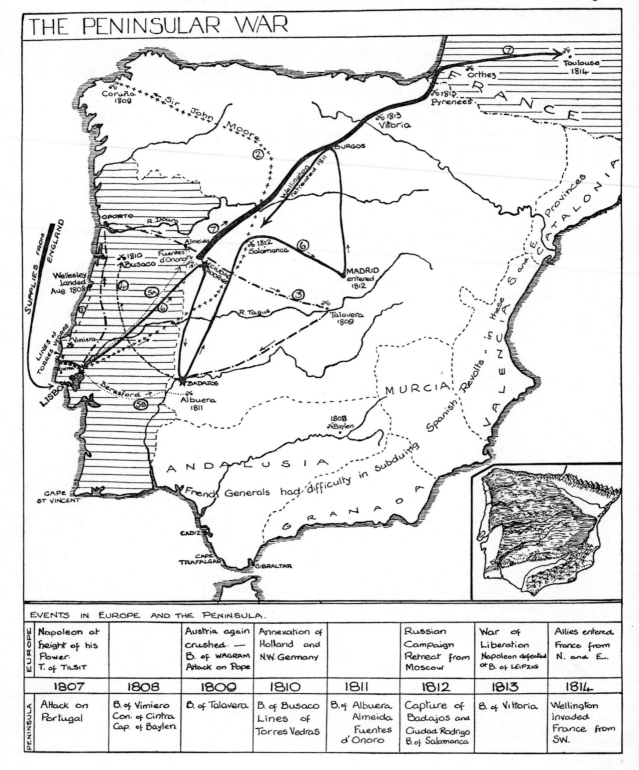

Map labels:
Coruña 1809 · Sir John Moore · FRANCE · Toulouse 1814 · Orthez · 1814 Pyrenees · 1813 Vitoria · BURGOS · Wellington retreated 1811 · OPORTO · R. Douro · Almeida · Fuentes d'Onoro · 1812 Salamanca · MADRID entered 1812 · Provinces · CATALONIA · Wellesley landed Aug. 1808 · 1810 Busaco · CIUDAD RODRIGO · SUPPLIES FROM ENGLAND · Vimiero · LINES of TORRES VEDRAS · R. Tague · Talavera 1809 · VALENCIA S. and · Spanish Revolts in these · LISBON · Beresford · BADAJOS · Albuera 1811 · MURCIA · 1808 Baylen · in subduing · French Generals had difficulty · ANDALUSIA · CAPE ST VINCENT · GRANADA · CADIZ · CAPE TRAFALGAR · GIBRALTAR

EVENTS IN EUROPE AND THE PENINSULA.							
EUROPE Napoleon at height of his Power. T. of Tilsit		Austria again crushed.— B. of Wagram Attack on Pope	Annexation of Holland and N.W. Germany		Russian Campaign Retreat from Moscow	War of Liberation Napoleon defeated at B. of Leipzig	Allies entered France from N. and E.
1807	**1808**	**1809**	**1810**	**1811**	**1812**	**1813**	**1814**
PENINSULA Attack on Portugal	B. of Vimiero Con. of Cintra Cap. of Baylen	B. of Talavera	B. of Busaco Lines of Torres Vedras	B. of Albuera Almeida Fuentes d'Onoro	Capture of Badajos and Ciudad Rodrigo B. of Salamanca	B. of Vittoria	Wellington invaded France from SW.

THE PENINSULAR WAR

A. CAUSES

(1) Napoleon, in order to compel Portugal to close its harbours to British ships, sent Junot to occupy Lisbon (1807).

(2) The Spaniards resented the passage of the French armies through their country, and when Napoleon forced their King to abdicate and appointed his brother, Joseph, King of Spain, they rose in revolt.

(3) The British Government sent an expedition under Wellesley to stiffen the resistance of both nations.

B. ADVANTAGES OF THE BRITISH IN THEIR STRUGGLE WITH THE FRENCH

(1) *The national resistance of the Spaniards.* The pride and patriotism of the Spaniards were aroused. The nation everywhere refused to accept defeat. Though the Spanish armies were unreliable in the field, irregular soldiers harassed the enemy by unceasing attacks. They cut off supplies and intercepted French troop reinforcements; they defended their towns with obstinate fury; and they organized revolt wherever a French garrison was stationed.

(2) *British command of the sea.* The British were able to secure supplies and reinforcements by sea. The French, on the other hand, had difficulty in maintaining communications in a land where roads were few and where deep valleys and high mountain chains made passage difficult. Owing to the poverty of the country and the irregular warfare of the Spaniards the French armies were starved.

(3) *Military skill of Wellington.* Patience, industry, and sure judgment were Wellington's chief qualities. He acted on the defensive from behind the lines of Torres Vedras until the weakness of the French gave him the opportunity to attack. Napoleon was forced to leave the campaign in the hands of rival generals, jealous of their reputation, and this divided control weakened the French.

(4) *Fighting qualities of the British army.* Though recruited from the roughest ranks, the army was disciplined by efficient leadership into the best and steadiest fighting force in Europe.

C. IMPORTANCE OF THE PENINSULAR WAR

(1) The long resistance of the Spaniards, unforeseen by Napoleon, was a steady drain on his resources. It compelled him to send his veteran troops to Spain when they were needed elsewhere.

(2) Spanish patriotism was an example for other nations.

DATE.	MAP REFERENCE.	NAPOLEONIC CAMPAIGNS IN EUROPE.	FRENCH CAMPAIGNS. In Peninsula.	BRITISH CAMPAIGNS. In Peninsula.
1808	I	Napoleon was at the height of his power after Tilsit, and Europe was under his domination.	Spaniards forced the French army to capitulate at Baylen. Spanish armies entered Madrid.	Wellesley drove the French from Portugal.
1808	II	He appointed his brother, Joseph, King of Spain, and occupied Madrid.	Soult, left in command, attacked Portugal.	Sir John Moore attempted to threaten Napoleon's communications in Spain, but was forced to retreat.
1809	III	War broke out between Austria and France. Napoleon withdrew from the Peninsula.	After the defeat of Austria (Wagram, 1809), the French armies were reinforced. Soult attacked and subjugated Andalusia.	Wellesley drove Soult out of Portugal back into Spain. (After his victory at Talavera, Wellesley was created Duke of Wellington.)
1810	IV	No military campaigns in Europe.	Massena, sent to reconquer Portugal, spent the winter in front of Torres Vedras, but was forced through starvation to retire.	Wellington retired behind the lines of Torres Vedras, having laid waste the country.
1811	V		French maintained their hold in Andalusia and Catalonia and conquered Valencia.	Wellington planned (but failed) to capture Ciudad Rodrigo and Badajoz—the two fortresses guarding the roads from Lisbon to Spain.
1812	VI	Napoleon embarked on Russian campaign.	After Salamanca, French gave up the attempt to hold the south and centre of Spain.	Wellington advanced into Spain and occupied Madrid, but later retreated into Portugal.
1813	VII	Napoleon was defeated in War of Liberation.	Only Catalonia remained in the hands of the French.	Wellington pushed across Spain to the foot of the Pyrenees.
1814	VII		Wellington's victorious advance into France.	

28

BRITISH ACQUISITIONS DURING THE NAPOLEONIC WARS

BEFORE the French Wars (1793–1815) the British Empire consisted of :
(*a*) A number of small islands in the West Indies.
(*b*) Newfoundland, Nova Scotia, and Canada.
(*c*) A few trading-posts in West Africa.
(*d*) Bombay, Madras, and Bengal in India.

The result of the American War of Independence had been the loss of more than half the Empire.

A. THE FRENCH WARS (1793–1815)

Britain was at war with the French Republic and Napoleon for more than twenty years. It was her policy to attack France and her allies, Spain and Holland, in their distant colonies, (*a*) to weaken their resistance in Europe, and (*b*) to secure new markets for the manufactures which Napoleon excluded from the Continent.

B. EFFECT OF THE WARS ON THE GROWTH OF THE BRITISH EMPIRE

At the end of the war Britain was without a rival as a colonial power.

(1) She had gained important strategic positions all over the world at the expense of France, Spain, and Holland.

(2) She had unchallenged supremacy on the seas.

(3) She was unhampered by opposition or commercial rivalry from the older colonizing countries.

(*a*) *France* had lost everything except a few West Indian Islands and trading-posts in India.

(*b*) *Holland* had suffered most of all ; she lost Cape Colony and Ceylon and the area now known as British Guiana. Britain restored Java to the Dutch at the end of the war, but in 1819 she secured the island of Singapore, which enabled her to compete with the Dutch in the trade of the East Indies and China.

(*c*) *Spain* and *Portugal* were powerless to subdue their rebellious colonies.

C. SUMMARY OF BRITISH GAINS (1814–1815)

(1) *By conquest during the wars : India.* The intrigues of the French with the native rulers in India led to a British attack on the lands of the ruler of Mysore. The necessity of keeping order caused Wellesley to secure control of Southern India and to extend the frontier in the North (see Map 29).

(2) *At the peace*

(*a*) *Trinidad, Tobago, and St Lucia.* These West Indian islands were particularly valuable for their plantation crops (sugar and tobacco) ; islands were regarded highly, as they were the most important centres of trade.

MAP 6

BRITISH ACQUISITIONS DURING NAPOLEONIC WARS

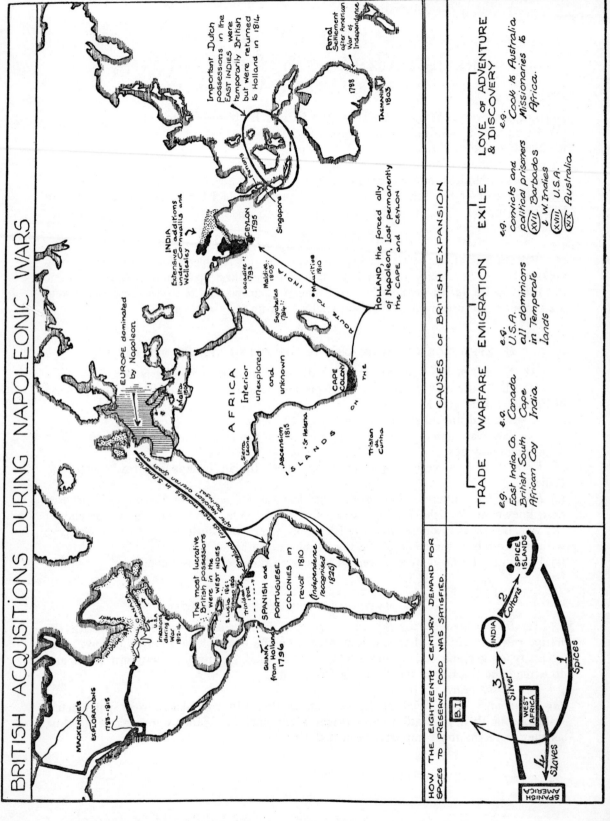

MACKENZIE'S EXPLORATIONS 1793-1815

CANADA

U.S.A. invasion during War 1812-14

The most lucrative British possessions were in the WEST INDIES

St. Lucia 1803, Tobago 1803, Trinidad

New troubles in S. America after Napoleon overran Spain & Portugal

GUIANA from Holland 1796

SPANISH and PORTUGUESE COLONIES in revolt 1810 (Independence recognised 1825)

EUROPE dominated by Napoleon

Malta 1800

Sierra Leone

Ascension 1815 · St. Helena

ISLANDS

Tristan da Cunha

AFRICA Interior unexplored and unknown

CAPE COLONY ON THE

Extensive additions under Cornwallis and Wellesley

INDIA

Laccadive 1793

Maldive 1905

Seychelles 1814

Mauritius 1810

ROUTE TO INDIA

CEYLON 1795

Singapore

Sumatra

Important Dutch possessions in the EAST INDIES were temporarily British but were returned to Holland in 1814

Penal Settlement after American War of Independence

1788

Tasmania 1803

HOLLAND, the forced ally of Napoleon, lost permanently the CAPE and CEYLON

(b) *Mauritius.* This island in the Indian Ocean was taken during the war, because the East Indian trade had suffered much from the damage caused by raiders using it as their base. It was not only an important strategic point but, like the West Indian possessions, had valuable sugar-plantations.

(c) *Ceylon.* This important possession was seized from the Dutch to secure the safety of India. It proved a useful market for British goods.

(d) *The Cape of Good Hope Colony.* A Dutch settlement, this colony at the southern tip of Africa was captured for use as a naval station on the route to the East ; it was retained because of its strategic value.

(e) *British Guiana.* Britain secured a foothold on the South American continent. (*N.B.* New markets in South America had helped Britain to survive Napoleon's Continental System.)

(f) *Malta.* This Mediterranean island became an important naval base. Since the opening of the Suez Canal its half-way position between Gibraltar and the canal has made it a vital link in Imperial communications (refer also Map 34).

(g) *Heligoland* (off the Elbe estuary) and *Ionian Islands* (off the shores of the Balkans). These islands were acquired to enable Britain to smuggle goods into the Continent. *N.B.* These islands are no longer British possessions.

MAP 7

ARTIFICIAL PROSPERITY DURING NAPOLEONIC WARS

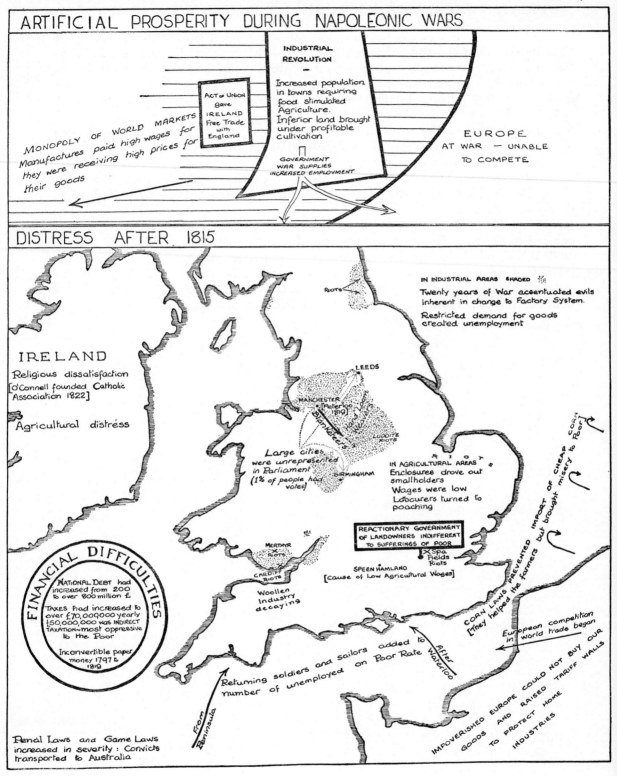

INDUSTRIAL REVOLUTION

Increased population in towns requiring food stimulated Agriculture.
Inferior land brought under profitable cultivation

ACT of UNION gave IRELAND Free Trade with England

MONOPOLY OF WORLD MARKETS Manufactures paid high wages for they were receiving high prices for their goods

GOVERNMENT WAR SUPPLIES INCREASED EMPLOYMENT

EUROPE AT WAR — UNABLE TO COMPETE

DISTRESS AFTER 1815

RIOTS

IN INDUSTRIAL AREAS SHADED
Twenty years of War accentuated evils inherent in change to Factory System.
Restricted demand for goods created unemployment

IRELAND
Religious dissatisfaction
[O'Connell founded Catholic Association 1822]

Agricultural distress

LEEDS

MANCHESTER [Peterloo 1819]

Low Corn Wages

LUDDITE RIOTS

Blanketeers

Large cities were unrepresented in Parliament (1% of people had votes)

BIRMINGHAM

RIOTS

IN AGRICULTURAL AREAS
Enclosures drove out smallholders
Wages were low
Labourers turned to poaching

REACTIONARY GOVERNMENT OF LANDOWNERS INDIFFERENT TO SUFFERINGS OF POOR

MERTHYR RIOTS

CARDIFF RIOTS

Woollen Industry decaying

Spa Fields Riots

SPEEN HAMLAND [Cause of Low Agricultural Wages]

CORN LAWS PREVENTED IMPORT OF CHEAP CORN [They helped the farmers but brought misery to Poor]

European competition in world trade began

IMPOVERISHED EUROPE COULD NOT BUY OUR GOODS AND RAISED TARIFF WALLS TO PROTECT HOME INDUSTRIES

FINANCIAL DIFFICULTIES
National Debt had increased from 200 to over 800 million £
Taxes had increased to over £70,000,000 yearly £50,000,000 was INDIRECT TAXATION—most oppressive to the Poor
Inconvertible paper money 1797 to 1819

Returning soldiers and sailors added to number of unemployed on Poor Rate
After Waterloo

From Peninsula

Penal Laws and Game Laws increased in severity: Convicts transported to Australia

ENGLAND IN 1815

THREE factors contributed to the misery and distress of the English people between 1815 and 1850:

(*a*) The changes of the Industrial and Agrarian Revolutions.
(*b*) The after-effects of the French Wars.
(*c*) The policy of the Government.

The Napoleonic Wars took place during the important period of transition from domestic to factory industry, and it is difficult to distinguish between the hardships caused by the economic changes and the wars. The wars caused more rapid changes and thus intensified the inevitable distress that such great transformations in industrial and agricultural methods must involve.

A. AGRICULTURE AND INDUSTRY

(1) *Effects of Agrarian Revolution.* The war years were a time of great prosperity to farmers and landlords. The importation of foreign corn was restricted by Napoleon's trade-war, and at the same time the home demand was increased by the development of industry. The new improved methods in agriculture were applied more readily, and a General Enclosure Act (1801) was passed to encourage their introduction. So keen was the demand for corn and so profitable the market that much unsuitable land was brought into cultivation.

The enclosure movement brought great distress to the small farmers (see Map 20 and notes on pp. 71-73). The wars added to their suffering. Prices were high, and wages remained low. The Berkshire Magistrates at Speenhamland in 1795 adopted a scale of relief to the labourer—whether employed or not—and this practice was generally adopted in agricultural areas. This system prevented a rise in wages.

When the war was over the period of artificial prosperity soon came to an end. Foreign corn could be imported more cheaply than British farmers could grow it. Many farmers were ruined. A series of bad harvests in the years after 1815 increased the difficulty of the farmers; the Corn Law of 1815 did not save many of them.

(2) *Effects of the Industrial Revolution.* The introduction of machinery brought great hardships to the workers in mines and factories; they were forced to work long hours in unwholesome surroundings at monotonous tasks for low wages. The hand-workers—craftsmen, whose skill was no longer required—lost status. The increased amount of capital required for a manufacturer to start in a factory industry condemned the majority to be wage-earners for the whole of their lives.

The rapid development of the new industries in the North and the Midlands, where no traditions of civic life existed, led to overcrowding in barrack-like towns, insanitary conditions, and the destruction of community life.

As production depended on the fluctuations of the market, work became more irregular; unemployment began to cast its shadow over the lives of wage-earners.

C

B. The French Wars

(1) *Effects of the Wars.* The war-needs stimulated production, especially in the metal and woollen industries. The dislocation of industry and trade on the Continent gave the British manufacturers a virtual monopoly of the markets of the world.

On the other hand, the Continental blockade interfered with trade and led to unemployment. Unemployed workmen in the Midlands and the North smashed machinery, believing that it was responsible for their miseries (Luddite Riots, 1811–1812). The cotton industry was affected by a stoppage of raw cotton during the war with America (1812–1814).

(2) *Post-war effects.*—The collapse of the market, when the Government's orders for arms and clothing ceased in 1815, dislocated the metal and woollen industries. The returning soldiers swelled the number of unemployed. Foreign customers were too impoverished to buy much.

C. The Policy of the Government

(1) *Finance.* Financial crises occurred several times during the period of the Revolutionary and Napoleonic Wars, *e.g.*, on their outbreak in 1793 and again in 1796 and 1797. Confidence in the country banks was undermined. When farmers, after a bad harvest, had to draw money from their banks, there was not enough ready cash available to meet their demand. The disasters of 1796 and the crisis of 1797 led to the suspension of payments by the Bank of England itself (*i.e.*, the bank no longer exchanged its notes for their face-value in gold).

The cost of the war was very considerable, especially as Britain financed the continental coalitions against Napoleon. Money was raised by loans ; taxes were high ; but Pitt's income-tax—introduced in 1797—was not continued after 1815. This meant that the burden of taxation fell more heavily on the poor than on the rich, for duties had to be levied on all articles of food and clothing. One-half of a workman's earnings went to the Government.

(2) *Repression.* The Parliament of 1815 did not represent the nation, but was dominated by the land-owning classes, who made no attempt to remedy the lot of the poor.

(a) The fear caused by the French Revolution in the minds of the ruling classes had not been allayed. Agitation for reforms was followed by repressive measures (*e.g.*, Six Acts of 1819, which seriously interfered with the liberty of the citizen). Workmen were prevented from taking united action to demand higher wages or better conditions by the enactment of the Combination Laws (1799–1800).

(b) The more thoughtful statesmen adopted the doctrine of free competition, or *laissez-faire*. In practice this meant that the working classes were at the mercy of the employers (see p. 46).

(c) The power of the landed interest in Parliament is shown in the passing of the Corn Laws in 1815, which prohibited the import of foreign corn until the price had reached 80s. a quarter. This was intended to enable the farmers to pay the high rents which had become current during the war ; actually bread became too dear for the working classes to buy.

CASTLEREAGH

CASTLEREAGH lived at a time of upheaval and war, and his outlook on life and politics was influenced thereby. As a young man he had seen lawlessness and revolution in Ireland. With a passionate belief that law and order were more essential than national freedom he had eagerly accepted and helped to carry out Pitt's plan of providing firm government by abolishing the separate parliament at Dublin. Later he had seen Europe convulsed by the Napoleonic Wars, and he strove to construct a political order which could preserve society from the destructive violence of revolution and war.

A. SECRETARY FOR WAR (1807–1809)

The mantle of Pitt, the organizer of opposition to Napoleon, fell on Castlereagh, who (a) supported the national rising in Spain and secured the appointment of Wellesley in the Peninsula, and (b) sent the ill-fated Walcheren expedition to the Netherlands.

B. FOREIGN SECRETARY (1812–1822)

(1) *Opposition to Napoleon.* As Foreign Secretary Castlereagh carried out successfully Pitt's plan of uniting Europe against Napoleon in the Fourth Coalition. He strove to make his allies realize that the downfall of the great disturber of the peace of Europe could only be brought about if each forgot selfish aims. This end he achieved at the Treaty of Chaumont (1814), whereby the allies undertook to continue together until Napoleon was defeated.

(2) *The Congress of Vienna and the resettlement of Europe.* Castlereagh's work at the Congress of Vienna :

(a) He tried to create a peace settlement that would endure. He realized that no lasting peace could be built on vengeful retaliations, and he used his influence and diplomatic skill to prevent the allies from imposing harsh terms.

(b) He transformed the fourth coalition into a permanent alliance. Alone in his generation he saw the vision of Europe at peace through the united efforts of the Great Powers.

(c) He preserved the trade and imperial interests of Britain, securing by purchase from Holland the Cape Colony and Ceylon. Most of the colonies of France and her enforced allies were returned, or compensation was paid for them.

(d) Stimulated by English public opinion he persuaded the Powers to abolish the slave-trade.

(3) *The United States of America.* The war between Great Britain and the U.S.A. (1812–1814) was the result of friction arising from the British blockade of the Napoleonic Empire. The war was ended by the Treaty of Ghent (1814), which left many questions unsettled. After the war Castlereagh established more friendly relations with the U.S.A. ; both countries agreed to withdraw warships from the Great Lakes, and in 1818 he negotiated the treaty that fixed the boundary between Canada and the U.S.A. along the forty-ninth parallel of latitude.

MAP 8

CASTLEREAGH

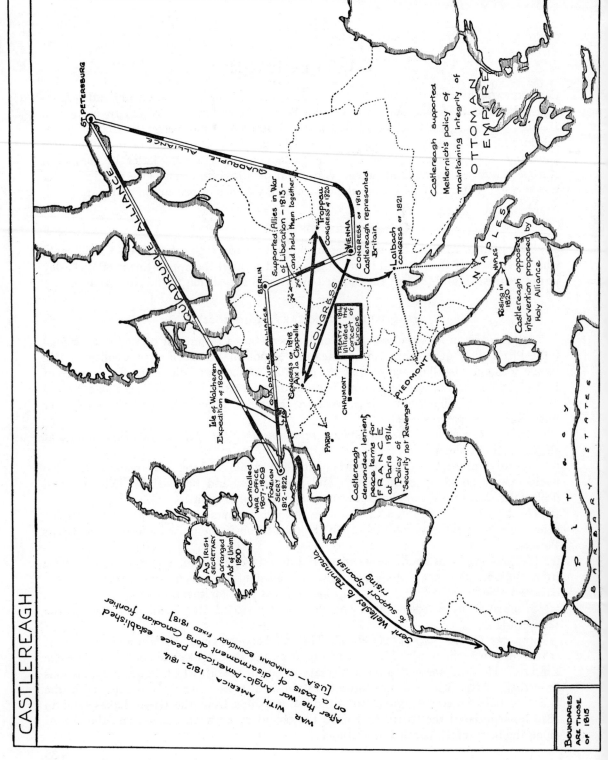

WAR WITH AMERICA 1812-1814.
After the war Anglo-American peace established
on a basis of disarmament along Canadian frontier
[U.S.A.—CANADIAN boundary fixed 1818]

As IRISH SECRETARY arranged Act of Union 1800

Controlled WAR OFFICE 1807-1809

FOREIGN SECRY 1812-1822

Isle of Walcheren Expedition of 1809

Sent Wellesley to Peninsula to support Spanish rising

PARIS

CHAUMONT

TREATY of 1814 initiated the Concert of Europe

CONGRESS of 1818 Aix la Chapelle

BERLIN

Supported Allies in War of Liberation – 1813 – and held them together

Troppau CONGRESS of 1820

VIENNA CONGRESS of 1815 Castlereagh represented Britain

Laibach CONGRESS of 1821

QUADRUPLE ALLIANCE

CONGRESS

ST PETERSBURG

Castlereagh demanded lenient peace terms for FRANCE at Paris 1814. Policy of 'Security not Revenge'

PIEDMONT

Rising in 1820 NAPLES

Castlereagh opposed intervention proposed by Holy Alliance

NAPLES

Castlereagh supported Metternich's policy of maintaining integrity of OTTOMAN EMPIRE

BARBARY STATES

(4) *The Concert of Europe* (1815–1822). Heedless of English public opinion, which deplored his association with despotic rulers, he determined to throw the weight of Britain into the preservation of peace in Europe. The Quadruple Alliance, born at Chaumont in 1814 as an instrument of war, might become, he believed, an association of the statesmen of the Great Powers for settling disputes. Instead of each sovereign state acting for itself, Castlereagh contemplated a federal council, or 'Concert of Europe.' For four years his project appeared to be succeeding.

At the Congress of Aix-la-Chapelle of 1818 European statesmen applauded his principles and carried out his proposals, which admitted France to the Concert of Europe.

In 1819, however, disorder and murmurs of discontent against oppression broke out in most European countries; in 1820 riots in Naples, Spain, and Portugal developed into rebellions for constitutional reform. To Metternich, the Chancellor of the Austrian Empire, these events heralded the breakdown of civilization, and he turned to the Concert of Europe as an instrument to preserve peace. Castlereagh, however, strongly disapproved of the use of the Concert to put down revolutions; he resisted the proposal to set up an international army, and protested against any intervention in the internal affairs of states. He believed that each country should retain the right to change its form of government as England had done in 1688; as the spokesman of a constitutional state, he refused to oppose the demands for constitutions abroad.

When Austria, Russia, and Prussia (the Holy Alliance) issued the Protocol of Troppau in 1820—a declaration of the right and duty of kings to help one another to preserve their despotic powers—Castlereagh saw the necessity of withdrawing from the Congress of Laibach, and with England's withdrawal came the ruin of his great project.

In 1822 Castlereagh and Metternich were almost reconciled; the latter for the moment saw advantages in non-intervention because he was suspicious of the Czar Alexander's ambitions in the Balkans and in Spain. A new congress was arranged at Verona for 1822, to deal with the Greek and Spanish revolutions; but Castlereagh did not attend. Worn out by public duties and private cares, his health failed. On his death the decision as to England's rôle in foreign affairs fell on his rival, Canning (refer Map 9, and notes on pp. 39–40).

MAP 9

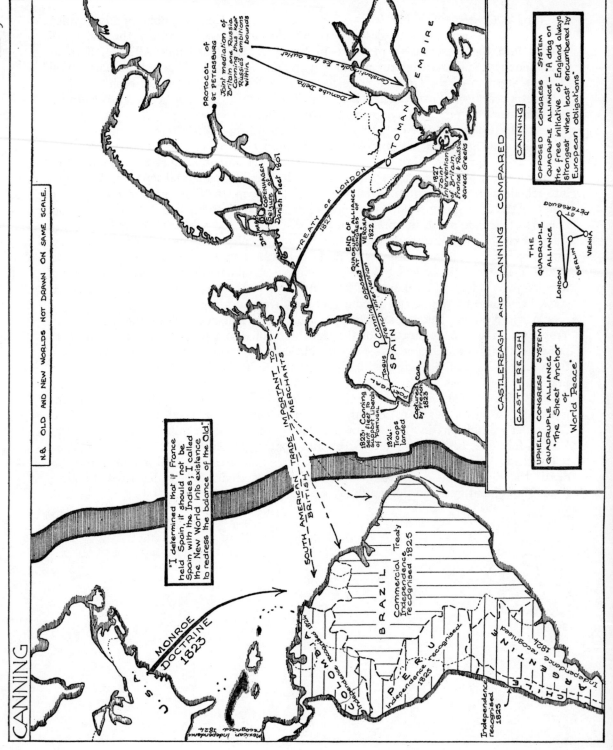

CANNING

N.B. OLD AND NEW WORLDS NOT DRAWN ON SAME SCALE.

MONROE DOCTRINE 1823

"I determined that if France held Spain, it should not be Spain with the Indies; I called the New World into existence to redress the balance of the Old."

U.S.

Mexican Independence recognised 1824.

COLOMBIA Independence recognised 1825

PERU Independence recognised 1825

BRAZIL Commercial Treaty Independence recognised 1825

CHILE Independence recognised 1825

ARGENTINA Independence recognised 1824

SOUTH AMERICAN TRADE IMPORTANT TO BRITISH MERCHANTS

Protocol of St. Petersburg

Joint mediation of Britain and Russia. Canning thus kept Russia's ambitions within bounds

Danube Delta

Constantinople — the free outlet

OTTOMAN EMPIRE

TREATY OF LONDON 1827

1827 Joint intervention of Britain, France & Russia Saved Greeks

END OF QUADRUPLE ALLIANCE Canning opposed CONGRESS OF VERONA 1822 French intervention

SPAIN

DENMARK COPENHAGEN Failure of Danish Fleet 1801

1823 Canning sent fleet to support Liberals of Portugal.

1824 Troops landed

R. Tagus

Trocadero

Captured by French 1823

CASTLEREAGH AND CANNING COMPARED

CASTLEREAGH

UPHELD CONGRESS SYSTEM QUADRUPLE ALLIANCE "The Sheet Anchor of World Peace"

THE QUADRUPLE ALLIANCE

London
Berlin
Vienna
St Petersburg

CANNING

OPPOSED CONGRESS SYSTEM QUADRUPLE ALLIANCE — "A drag on the free initiative of England always strongest when least encumbered by European obligations"

CANNING

LIKE Castlereagh, Canning had lived through the stormy period of revolution; he pursued the main lines of his predecessor's policy and contended against the despotism of the Holy Alliance, which he regarded as dangerous to the states of Europe. He favoured constitutional government, but objected to interference with the institutions of other countries, whether by democrats or by despots. Great Britain, he believed, should be isolated from European affairs unless by interference some advantage to this country could be gained.

A. FOREIGN SECRETARY (1807–1809)

The years when he was first Foreign Minister were perhaps the most serious in the long struggle with Napoleon.

Napoleon had inaugurated his Continental System and made his alliance with Alexander I at Tilsit. The two emperors had agreed to force Denmark to join them in opposition to Britain, as the Danish fleet was necessary for the success of the trade war. Canning, receiving secret information, sent an expedition to Copenhagen. The city was bombarded and the Danish fleet seized. Napoleon was baulked, but Canning's attack on a neutral country is difficult to justify.

B. FOREIGN SECRETARY (1822–1827): PRIME MINISTER (1827)

Canning became Foreign Secretary just as the Congress was to meet at Verona to settle the affairs of Spain. Unlike Castlereagh, he had no belief in the power of the Congress System to preserve the peace of Europe. Like Castlereagh, he was opposed to interference in the internal affairs of other states ("except in great emergencies, and then with a commanding force").

The Holy Alliance (Austria, Russia, Prussia) fearful of the disorder that was gaining ground in Spain, agreed that France should send an army to restore the power of the Spanish King, who had been forced by the liberals to grant a constitution. Canning strongly opposed this action and, after this, refused to act in concert with the other Powers; the system of congresses came to an end, unable to survive without the support of Great Britain.

Canning's work was mainly concerned with international relations arising out of troubles with Portugal, the Spanish colonies, and Greece.

(1) *Portugal*
(a) 1823. By sending a fleet to the mouth of the Tagus, Canning supported the liberals in Portugal and made the throne secure for the King.
(b) 1825. He used his influence to effect a peaceful separation between Portugal and her colony, Brazil, and recognized its independence in 1825.
(c) 1826. When civil war broke out he sent troops to help the liberals on the grounds that Spain was supplying arms.

(2) *The Spanish American colonies.* The Spanish colonies had been in revolt

since 1807, and their independence was almost assured. There was a danger that Spain would recover control with the aid of the French. When a French army occupied Cadiz in 1823, Canning intimated that Britain would oppose any attempt to coerce the revolting colonists. He was concerned for British trade and wanted an ' open market ' for British goods in South America.

President Monroe announced, in a message to Congress, that the U.S.A. would not tolerate interference by European Powers in the continent of America. Canning had invited U.S. co-operation, but he realized that the President's statement was a declaration of American power and was directed as much against Britain as against any other European state. Nevertheless, Monroe's support (the ' Monroe doctrine ') had a great moral effect in Europe.

In 1824 Canning recognized the independence of the Spanish American colonies and made commercial treaties with them. At the back of his diplomacy was the desire to secure the support of the South American states to counterbalance the power of the U.S.A.

(3) *The Greek War of Independence.* The Greeks revolted against the Turks in 1821. All the European Powers were interested. Alexander I of Russia, as head of the Greek Church, was anxious to support his fellow Christians ; but as the ally of Metternich in opposition to revolution, he feared the effects of such action. England, France, and Austria were afraid of the intervention of Russia.

When Canning came to power he was faced with a difficult problem. The British public sympathized with the Greeks and wanted the Government to help them. Canning was strictly neutral at first.

In 1825 the situation changed. Nicholas I, now Czar, was determined to take action ; the Sultan had gained the support of his powerful vassal, Mehemet Ali of Egypt, and the Greeks were in danger of extermination. They asked for British protection. Canning determined at all costs to prevent Russia from acting alone, and he invited the Powers to a Congress in London in 1827. It was agreed to offer mediation in the quarrel ; Greece was to be a self-governing state, paying tribute to the Sultan. It was also agreed secretly to send an expedition to enforce the armistice.

Canning died before the plan was carried out. The combined fleets of Britain, France, and Russia destroyed the Turkish fleet at Navarino in 1827, and Greek independence was assured.

PARLIAMENTARY REFORM

FROM the eighteenth century until after the Great War of 1914–1918, the British constitution, with its Parliament, was admired, envied, and even copied by the nations of Europe; in foreign eyes it was clearly a highly successful form of government, because the power of Great Britain had increased so greatly; no revolutions occurred, yet it afforded a remarkable degree of freedom to its citizens.

The most striking characteristic of the constitution since the 'Glorious Revolution' of 1688 has been the rise of the power of the assembly representing the nation—*i.e.*, the House of Commons. Although the House of Commons claimed to speak for the people, it is clear from Map 10 that it has not always been fully representative of the nation as a whole.

Few changes had been made in the Parliamentary system since the time of Cromwell. Abuses were attacked in the eighteenth century, but the movement for reform, encouraged by the French Revolution, was checked by Pitt's Government, which feared that political agitation would result in revolutionary disorder.

The demand for reform was revived after 1815, when the working classes, led to believe that Parliamentary reform would put an end to their miseries, united with the unenfranchized middle classes to wrest political power from the land-owning class.

A. THE NEED FOR REFORM: THE ELECTORAL SYSTEM BEFORE 1832

(1) *Inequality in size and distribution of constituencies.* The map shows that all Members of Parliament did not represent an equal number of electors.

(*a*) Compared with England, Wales and Scotland were inadequately represented.

(*b*) In England (and to a greater extent in Scotland) a redistribution of seats was necessary to adjust Parliamentary representation to the changed distribution of population that had been caused by the Industrial Revolution.

(i) The *counties* sent two Members to Parliament, as in the thirteenth century, irrespective of their different sizes or density of population.

(ii) The *boroughs* sent most members. They were not all large towns; many of them had never even been populous villages (Tudor nomination boroughs), and some were not even hamlets (*cf.* Old Sarum). Not all boroughs (*i.e.*, towns which had mayors and corporations) were represented, but only those which had returned members from the time of James I.

(*c*) The landed gentry influenced both county and borough elections, thus controlling the House of Commons as they did the House of Lords.

(i) There were *pocket*, or *nomination*, boroughs, in which the landowner was the patron, and he had the absolute right to choose the members.

(ii) In the *rotten* boroughs there were voters, but direct bribery (*i.e.*, money) or indirect bribery (*e.g.*, the landlord might raise the rent of his tenant) enabled the patron to secure control.

(iii) The county voters were more independent of the gentry than those in the

MAP 10

PARLIAMENTARY REFORM 1832

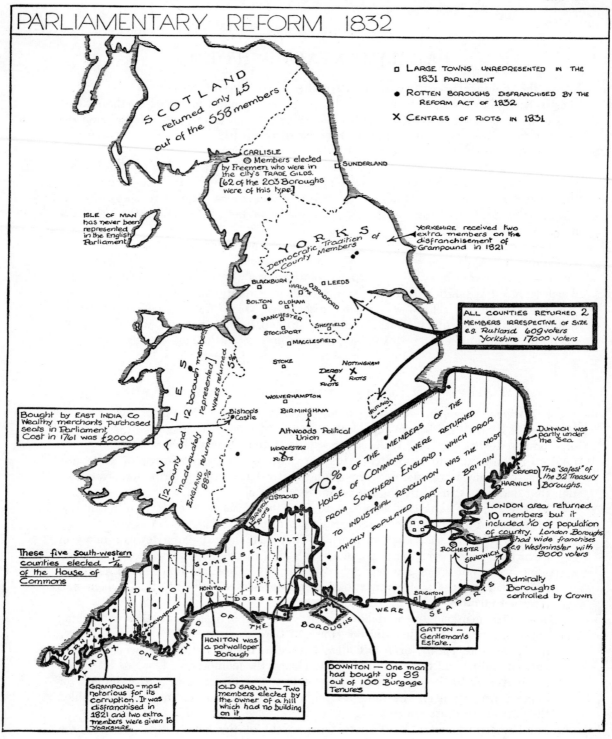

□ LARGE TOWNS UNREPRESENTED IN THE 1831 PARLIAMENT

● ROTTEN BOROUGHS DISFRANCHISED BY THE REFORM ACT OF 1832

X CENTRES OF RIOTS IN 1831

SCOTLAND returned only 45 out of the 558 members

CARLISLE
Members elected by Freemen who were in the city's TRADE GILDS.
[62 of the 203 Boroughs were of this type]

SUNDERLAND

ISLE OF MAN has never been represented in the English Parliament

Y O R K S
Democratic Tradition of County Members

YORKSHIRE received two extra members on the disfranchisement of Grampound in 1821

ALL COUNTIES RETURNED 2 MEMBERS IRRESPECTIVE OF SIZE e.g. Rutland 609 voters Yorkshire 17000 voters

BLACKBURN   LEEDS
HALIFAX   BRADFORD
BOLTON   OLDHAM
MANCHESTER
STOCKPORT   SHEFFIELD
MACCLESFIELD
STOKE

W A L E S
[12 county and 12 borough members]
5%
inadequately
WALES returned
represented
ENGLAND returned 88%

Bought by EAST INDIA Co Wealthy merchants purchased seats in Parliament. Cost in 1761 was £2000

Bishop's Castle

NOTTINGHAM X RIOTS
DERBY X RIOTS

WOLVERHAMPTON
BIRMINGHAM
Attwoods Political Union

RUTLAND

WORCESTER X RIOTS

70% OF THE MEMBERS OF THE HOUSE OF COMMONS WERE RETURNED FROM SOUTHERN ENGLAND, WHICH PRIOR TO INDUSTRIAL REVOLUTION WAS THE MOST THICKLY POPULATED PART OF BRITAIN

DUNWICH was partly under the Sea

ORFORD   The "safest" of the 32 Treasury Boroughs.
HARWICH

LONDON area returned 10 members but it included 1/10 of population of country. London Boroughs had wide franchises e.g. Westminster with 9000 voters

These five south-western counties elected 1/4 of the House of Commons

BRISTOL RIOTS   STROUD
WILTS
SOMERSET
DEVON
HONITON
DORSET
CORNWALL ALMOST ONE THIRD OF THE BOROUGHS
DEVONPORT
BRIGHTON

ROCHESTER
SANDWICH
WERE SEAPORTS

Admiralty Boroughs controlled by Crown

GATTON — A Gentleman's Estate.

HONITON was a potwalloper Borough

DOWNTON — One man had bought up 99 out of 100 Burgage Tenures

GRAMPOUND — most notorious for its corruption. It was disfranchised in 1821 and two extra members were given to YORKSHIRE.

OLD SARUM — Two members elected by the owner of a hill which had no building on it.

boroughs (*N.B.* the Yorkshire freeholders) ; nevertheless, they were not free from pressure.

(*d*) *Unrepresented towns.* As a result of the Industrial Revolution the population of the coal- and iron-fields of the Midlands and North grew rapidly. In these areas there had been few boroughs. Nearly all the rotten boroughs were in the South. Manchester, Leeds, and Birmingham had become great cities but sent no representatives to Parliament.

(2) *Lack of uniformity in qualifications for the franchise.* The map shows that not one man in a hundred had the right to vote ; not only was the franchise limited, but there was no uniform plan. The qualifications for the franchise had been different in county and borough since the Middle Ages and continued so until 1885.

(*a*) *In the county.* In the counties the forty-shilling freeholder had a right to vote. (*N.B.* Freeholders alone had the franchise—because the rest had been serfs in the Middle Ages. Leaseholders, for example, were excluded, so a man who had bought land worth forty shillings a year could vote, but the man who paid £40 a year in rent could not.)

(*b*) *In the boroughs.* There was no uniform qualification ; the right to vote varied according to ancient custom :

(i) *Burgage boroughs* were those where the right to vote attached to some particular building or plot of land (*e.g.*, Old Sarum ; there was a tendency for this type to become pocket boroughs).

(ii) *Scot and lot boroughs* were those in which the franchise depended on the payment of some local tax or rates. Generally all the householders had a vote (*e.g.*, Penrhyn).

(iii) *Potwalloper boroughs* were very similar. Every occupier of a room containing a fireplace on which a pot could be boiled had a vote (*e.g.*, Honiton). Thus the working classes were represented in scot and lot and potwalloper boroughs.

(iv) *Corporation boroughs* were those where voting was limited to members of the Corporation. (*N.B.* Before the Municipal Corporations Act of 1835 the Corporations were even less representative of the citizens than the House of Commons was of the nation.)

(v) *Freemen boroughs* were the largest and most independent group. In these the freemen—generally members of the trade gilds—had the right to vote. Corrupt practices occurred (*e.g.*, at Grampound) when the Corporation nominated honorary freemen.

Note

An election was a source of profit to :

(*a*) Electors—who often sold their votes.

(*b*) Owners of rotten boroughs—who sold seats to the highest bidders.

(*c*) M.P.'s—whose votes in Parliament could be sold for Honours and positions.

(3) *Unfair system of voting.* Another weakness was that elections were held under a system of open voting. Disorderly scenes were frequent. It was not uncommon for candidates to bribe the mob as well as the electors so as to make independent voting difficult.

MAP II

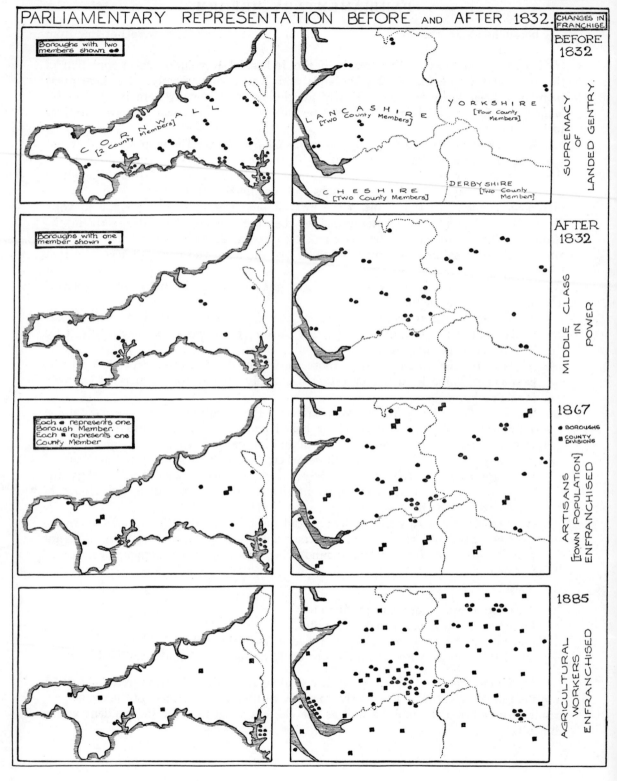

PARLIAMENTARY REPRESENTATION BEFORE AND AFTER 1832.

CHANGES IN FRANCHISE

BEFORE 1832 — SUPREMACY OF LANDED GENTRY.

Boroughs with two members shown ●●

C O R N W A L L [2 County Members]

L A N C A S H I R E [Two County Members]   Y O R K S H I R E [Four County Members]

C H E S H I R E [Two County Members]   D E R B Y S H I R E [Two County Member]

AFTER 1832 — MIDDLE CLASS IN POWER.

Boroughs with one member shown ●

1867 — ARTISANS [TOWN POPULATION] ENFRANCHISED.

Each ● represents one Borough Member.
Each ■ represents one County Member

● BOROUGHS
■ COUNTY DIVISIONS

1885 — AGRICULTURAL WORKERS ENFRANCHISED.

B. CIRCUMSTANCES WHICH AIDED THE REFORM MOVEMENT AND LED TO THE
PASSING OF THE REFORM BILL OF 1832

(1) Most important was the growth of a wealthy middle class—manufacturers, merchants, and professional people, who were interested in good government and wanted to share in the making of laws. They slowly began to realize the value of political power.

(2) The impoverished working classes, discontented with their lot, were led to believe by their radical leaders (*e.g.*, Cobbett and Orator Hunt) that conditions would improve if a reform of Parliament gave them a right to vote.

(3) The Whig Party advocated reform, hoping to secure the support of the middle class and so to overthrow the Tories.

(4) The July Revolution of 1830 in France resulted in the setting up of a Parliamentary Government controlled by the middle class. This strengthened the agitation for reform in England.

(5) King William IV was more ready to accept the idea of reform than his predecessor, George IV.

Map 11 shows the changes in Parliamentary representation which followed the Reform Bills of 1832, 1867, and 1885 in two strongly contrasting areas :
(*a*) *Cornwall*—over-represented before the Act of 1832, largely because of the creation of boroughs by the Tudor monarchs.
(*b*) *Northern Counties*—most thickly populated and rapidly growing areas, which had few representatives before 1832.

The table on p. 48 summarizes the changes made by successive Reform Bills during the nineteenth century, resulting in greater uniformity of electoral areas and a wider enfranchisement of the people.

MAP 12

REFORM   I

THE INDUSTRIAL REVOLUTION PRODUCED A NEW MANUFACTURING CLASS WHOSE COMMERCIAL DOCTRINE WAS LAISSEZ FAIRE. THIS INVOLVED THE SWEEPING AWAY OF RESTRICTIONS ON THE FREEDOM OF TRADE AND INDUSTRY

THE REFORMS WERE DUE TO

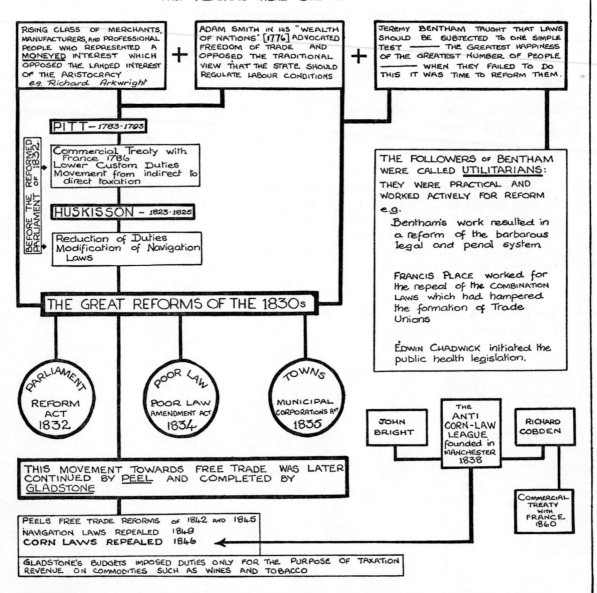

RISING CLASS OF MERCHANTS, MANUFACTURERS, AND PROFESSIONAL PEOPLE WHO REPRESENTED A MONEYED INTEREST WHICH OPPOSED THE LANDED INTEREST OF THE ARISTOCRACY
e.g. Richard Arkwright

+

ADAM SMITH IN HIS "WEALTH OF NATIONS" [1776] ADVOCATED FREEDOM OF TRADE AND OPPOSED THE TRADITIONAL VIEW THAT THE STATE SHOULD REGULATE LABOUR CONDITIONS

+

JEREMY BENTHAM TAUGHT THAT LAWS SHOULD BE SUBJECTED TO ONE SIMPLE TEST —— THE GREATEST HAPPINESS OF THE GREATEST NUMBER OF PEOPLE —— WHEN THEY FAILED TO DO THIS IT WAS TIME TO REFORM THEM.

BEFORE THE REFORMED PARLIAMENT OF 1832.

PITT — 1783-1793

Commercial Treaty with France 1786
Lower Custom Duties
Movement from indirect to direct taxation

HUSKISSON — 1823-1825

Reduction of Duties
Modification of Navigation Laws

THE FOLLOWERS OF BENTHAM WERE CALLED UTILITARIANS:
THEY WERE PRACTICAL AND WORKED ACTIVELY FOR REFORM
e.g.
Bentham's work resulted in a reform of the barbarous legal and penal system

FRANCIS PLACE worked for the repeal of the COMBINATION LAWS which had hampered the formation of Trade Unions

EDWIN CHADWICK initiated the public health legislation.

THE GREAT REFORMS OF THE 1830s

PARLIAMENT
REFORM ACT 1832

POOR LAW
POOR LAW AMENDMENT ACT 1834

TOWNS
MUNICIPAL CORPORATIONS ACT 1835

JOHN BRIGHT

THE ANTI CORN-LAW LEAGUE founded in MANCHESTER 1838

RICHARD COBDEN

THIS MOVEMENT TOWARDS FREE TRADE WAS LATER CONTINUED BY PEEL AND COMPLETED BY GLADSTONE

COMMERCIAL TREATY WITH FRANCE 1860

PEEL'S FREE TRADE REFORMS OF 1842 AND 1845
NAVIGATION LAWS REPEALED 1849
CORN LAWS REPEALED 1846

GLADSTONE'S BUDGETS IMPOSED DUTIES ONLY FOR THE PURPOSE OF TAXATION REVENUE ON COMMODITIES SUCH AS WINES AND TOBACCO

LAISSEZ FAIRE WAS A GREAT SUCCESS: ENGLAND'S INDUSTRY, TRADE, AND WEALTH GREW RAPIDLY SHE BECAME THE MOST POWERFUL AND INFLUENTIAL COUNTRY IN THE WORLD.

MAP 13

REFORM   II

THE INDUSTRIAL REVOLUTION ENTAILED COMPLETE CHANGES IN SOCIAL CONDITIONS: WHILE THE MANUFACTURERS GREW WEALTHY THE POOR LIVED IN OVERCROWDED AND INSANITARY HOUSES THEY WERE ILL PAID AND OVERWORKED THE LAISSEZ FAIRE ATTITUDE OF THE GOVERNMENT FAILED TO SATISFY THEM REFORMERS POINTED OUT THAT IN PRACTICE IT MEANT THE OPPRESSION OF THE POOR

THESE HUMANITARIAN REFORMERS INCLUDED

ROMANTICS	REVOLUTIONARIES	RADICALS	SOCIALISTS	PHILANTHROPISTS
e.g. the Poets Burns & Wordsworth "Le coeur aussi a ses raisons"	e.g. Paine & Godwin presented lofty ideals of the dignity of man.	e.g. Wm Cobbett founded a weekly Journal – "THE POLITICAL REGISTER & Major Cartwright founded Hampden Clubs	e.g. Robert Owen considered a man's character depended on his environment and to improve mankind he advocated reform	e.g. Wm Wilberforce attacked slavery Shaftesbury attacked evils of child labour in factories

THE GOVERNMENT LARGELY IGNORED THE EARLY AGITATORS BECAUSE:

A: THEY ACCEPTED THE ECONOMISTS' DOCTRINE THAT WAGES COULD NOT BE RAISED OR HOURS OF LABOUR REDUCED WITHOUT DISASTER TO BOTH EMPLOYER AND EMPLOYEE

B: THEY BELIEVED, WITH MALTHUS, THAT AN IMPROVED STANDARD OF LIVING WOULD LEAD TO A TOO RAPID INCREASE IN THE POPULATION AND THAT PHILANTHROPIC EFFORT THEREFORE WAS FUTILE AND DANGEROUS.

THE REACTION FROM LAISSEZ FAIRE

WAS COMPLETE IN THE SECOND HALF OF THE 19TH CENTURY

LITERARY INFLUENCES
Mid-Victorian literature thoroughly opposed LAISSEZ FAIRE
e.g. Novelists —
Dickens : Reade
Poet: Browning

INTERNATIONAL RIVALRY
1 State Socialism
e.g. Bismarck
2 Growth of Foreign competition and introduction of Protective Tariffs
3 New Imperial Policy fostered colonial preference

GROWTH OF SOCIALISM

CHRISTIAN SOCIALISTS	LITERARY SOCIALISTS	SCIENTIFIC SOCIALISTS
e.g. Kingsley regarded LAISSEZ FAIRE as contra-dictory to Christian principles	e.g. Ruskin & Morris objected to the social injustices and ugliness of modern industry	e.g. Karl Marx emphasized the materialist outlook on life

PROMOTION OF INDUSTRIAL WELFARE
e.g.
FACTORY ACTS
MINES ACTS
WORKMEN'S COMPENSATION ACTS
TRUCK ACTS

REGULATION OF TRADE AND INDUSTRY
e.g.
RAILWAY REGULATION ACTS
MERCHANT SHIPPING ACTS
MERCHANDISE MARKS ACTS

PROMOTION OF SOCIAL WELFARE
e.g
EDUCATION GRANTS
PUBLIC HEALTH ACTS
HOUSING & TOWN PLANNING ACTS
PRISON REFORM
NATIONAL HEALTH & UNEMPLOYMENT INSURANCE ACTS

THE HISTORY OF SOCIAL AND INDUSTRIAL LEGISLATION DURING THE LATTER PART OF THE 19TH CENTURY IS ONE OF EVER-INCREASING CONTROL OVER THE FREEDOM OF MANUFACTURERS.

THE CRITICISM OF SOCIAL REFORMERS AND SOCIALISTS GRADUALLY ALTERED PUBLIC OPINION AND BY THE END OF THE CENTURY THE RESPONSIBILITY OF THE STATE FOR SOCIAL AND INDUSTRIAL CONDITIONS WAS GENERALLY RECOGNISED

C. Parliamentary Reforms during Nineteenth Century: Summary of Changes

Date	Electoral Area		Qualification for Franchise		No. of Voters	No. of Voters to Population: One in
	County	Borough	County	Borough		
Before 1832.	Every county represented by two members	Boroughs—usually sending two members—were mainly situated in South of England.	Freeholders of land worth 40s. a year.	A variety of qualifications.	500,000	50
After Act of Grey, 1832.	Larger counties gained more representatives.	56 rotten boroughs lost representation. New towns enfranchised.	Richer tenants (£50 leaseholders) as well as freeholders.	Householders who paid £10 a year in rent and rates.	1,000,000	24
After Act of Disraeli, 1867.	Larger counties gained more representation.	More small boroughs disfranchised, and more representatives given to larger towns.	Tenants who paid £12 a year rent added.	All householders and lodgers who paid £10 a year for unfurnished rooms.	2,500,000	12
After Act of Gladstone, 1884–1885.	Counties divided into constituencies containing approximately the same number of voters as the boroughs.	More equalization.	All householders and lodgers who paid £10 a year for unfurnished rooms.		8,500,000	7
After Act of 1918.	More equal electoral areas.		All men over 21 years of age and all women over 30 years of age.		16,500,000	3

ENGLAND AND THE CRIMEAN WAR

THIS is the only big European war of the nineteenth century in which Britain took part; it resulted from the weakness of Turkey and the ambition of Russia to expand at her expense.

A. CAUSES OF THE WAR

(1) As a result of a disagreement between the Latin and Greek Christians in Palestine regarding the Holy Places, discussions later arose about the position of Christians in other parts of the Turkish Empire. The Czar, Nicholas I, claimed the right to protect the Christian subjects in Turkey.

(2) The French Emperor, Napoleon III, was personally antagonistic to Nicholas, eager to secure the confidence of the Roman Catholics in France, and not unwilling to gain prestige in the event of war.

(3) British statesmen were divided as to the policy they should adopt. Lord Aberdeen wanted peace. Palmerston, suspicious of Nicholas I, who had suggested in 1853 that " Turkey was a sick man at the point of death " and that her empire should be partitioned, favoured opposition to Russia. It was this division of counsel in the Cabinet that caused Great Britain to drift into war and encouraged both Russia and Turkey to refuse concessions.

(4) Turkey rejected Russia's claim and war broke out between them.

(5) Russian ships destroyed a Turkish squadron off Sinope in the Black Sea.

(6) The British public, hating the tyranny of the Czar, forced the Government to act on behalf of Turkey.

B. THE CAMPAIGNS

The Allies, France and Britain, declared war on Russia in 1854. The Russians had already crossed the River Pruth and had invaded Turkish territory.

Britain and France planned to attack the Russian naval base of Sebastopol, in the Crimean Peninsula, where the navy could advantageously co-operate with the army as it had done in the Peninsular War.

The siege of Sebastopol (1854–1855). The allied troops landed at Eupatoria, marched southward, and defeated a Russian force near the River Alma. Instead of attacking Sebastopol immediately, they encamped to the south of the city. The Russians hastily threw up fortifications and blocked the mouth of the harbour by sinking old ships.

The Allies were unable completely to encircle the town; reinforcements could enter, and the Russians could make sorties—as they did (unsuccessfully) at Balaclava and Inkerman.

The siege was therefore long and difficult; it lasted over a year, and during the winter the sufferings of the troops increased. Owing to mismanagement the transport service was inefficient, and clothing, food, and equipment were inadequate. Hospital arrangements were a scandal.

D

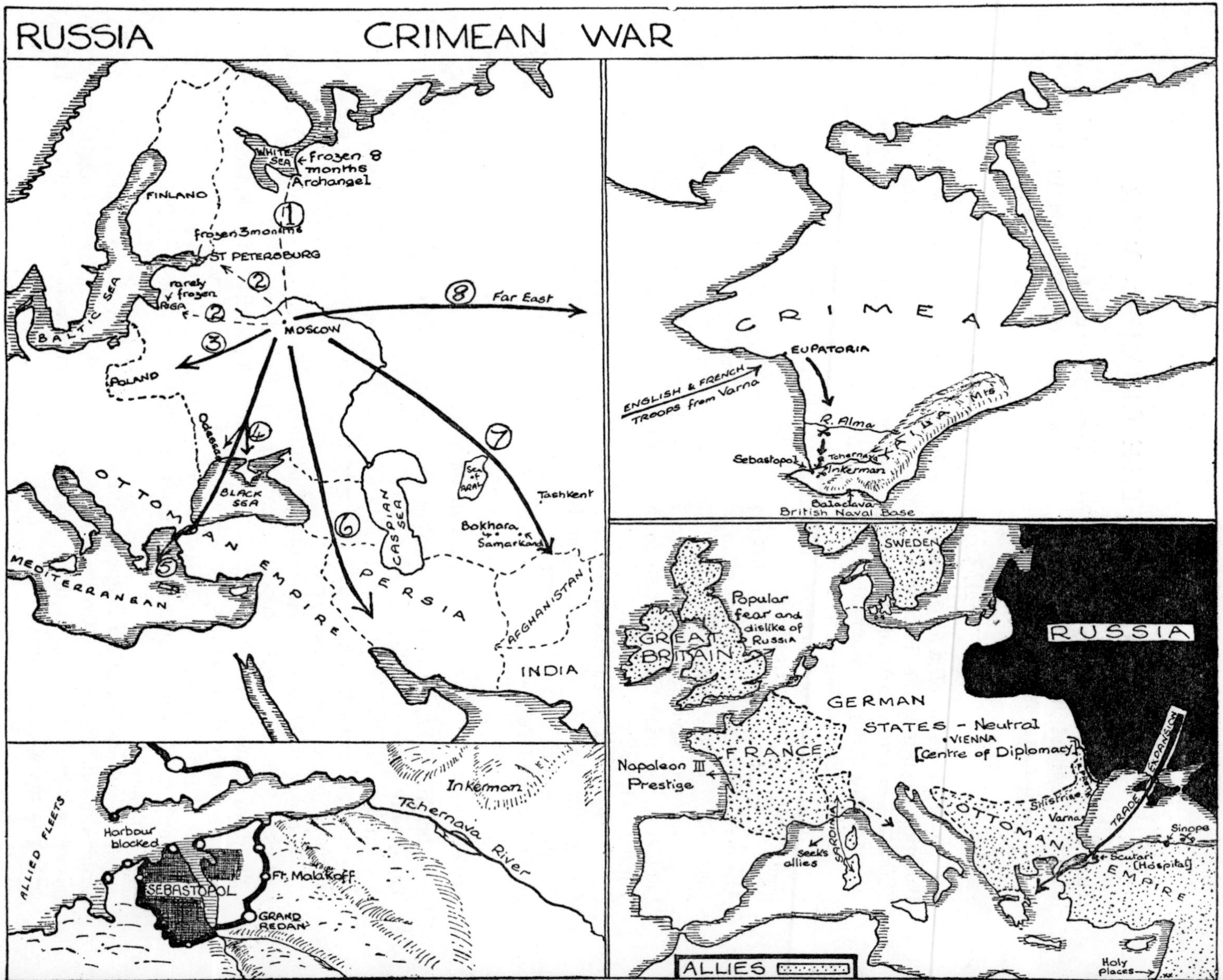

MAP 14

CRIMEAN WAR

RUSSIA

FINLAND

BALTIC SEA

White Sea frozen 8 months
Archangel

Frozen 3 months

ST PETERSBURG

rarely frozen sea

POLAND

Odessa

MOSCOW

BLACK SEA

① ② ② ③ ④ ⑤ ⑥ ⑦ ⑧

Far East

OTTOMAN EMPIRE

MEDITERRANEAN

CASPIAN SEA

Khiva

Bokhara Samarkand

Tashkent

AFGHANISTAN

PERSIA

INDIA

Tchernaya River

Inkerman

SEBASTOPOL

Ft. Malakoff

GRAND REDAN

Harbour blocked

ALLIED FLEETS

CRIMEA

EUPATORIA

R. Alma

Alma
Balaclava
Inkerman

Sebastopol

Balaclava British Naval Base

ENGLISH & FRENCH
TROOPS from Varna

CRIMEA

MTS

SWEDEN

GREAT BRITAIN

Popular fear and dislike of Russia

FRANCE

Napoleon III Prestige

GERMAN STATES – Neutral
VIENNA
[Centre of Diplomacy]

Varna
Seat's allies

RUSSIA

OTTOMAN EMPIRE

TRADE

KARS

Batoum

Silistria

Varna

Sinope
Sinope (Hospital)

Holy places

ALLIES

ENGLAND AND THE CRIMEAN WAR

In 1855 the Russian army withdrew from Sebastopol, after assaults had been made by the French on the Malakoff Fort and by the British (unsuccessfully) on the Redan.

C. THE TREATY OF PARIS (1856)

By this treaty the Allies apparently secured the objects for which they had fought. Turkey remained intact ; Russia was denied all rights over the Christian subjects of the Turk ; and only Turkish warships were permitted to pass through the Straits.

Yet Russia remained a menace to Britain. The war was waged in vain against the restless ambition of Russia, which turned eastward towards Persia and Afghanistan (refer to Maps 15, 16, and 17). Even in Europe Russia was still a danger, and during the Franco-Prussian War of 1870 her warships passed through the straits into the Black Sea. British statesmen had to agree to a revision of the Treaty of Paris.

D. RESULTS OF THE WAR FOR BRITAIN

(1) *The Army.* The flagrant weaknesses of the administration of the British army had been exposed ; the necessity for one supreme authority was clear. Army reforms were introduced by Gladstone's Government in 1870–1871.

(2) *Hospital reform.* Permanent changes were made in the Army Medical Service as a result of Florence Nightingale's work during the war. Civil hospitals were also improved. The Red Cross Movement also developed as a result of her influence.

(3) *Maritime code in war.* International regulations were drawn up for the protection of neutrals in time of war. This code affected Britain, the greatest naval power, more than any other nation.

(4) *British politics.* Lord Aberdeen's conduct of the war was severely criticized, and he resigned in 1855. Palmerston returned to power and remained the dominant influence in British politics until his death in 1865 (see Map 15).

(5) *India.* Troops were withdrawn from India during the war, and this affected the situation in India. The discontented native soldiers had a better chance of success when they revolted in 1857.

MAP 15

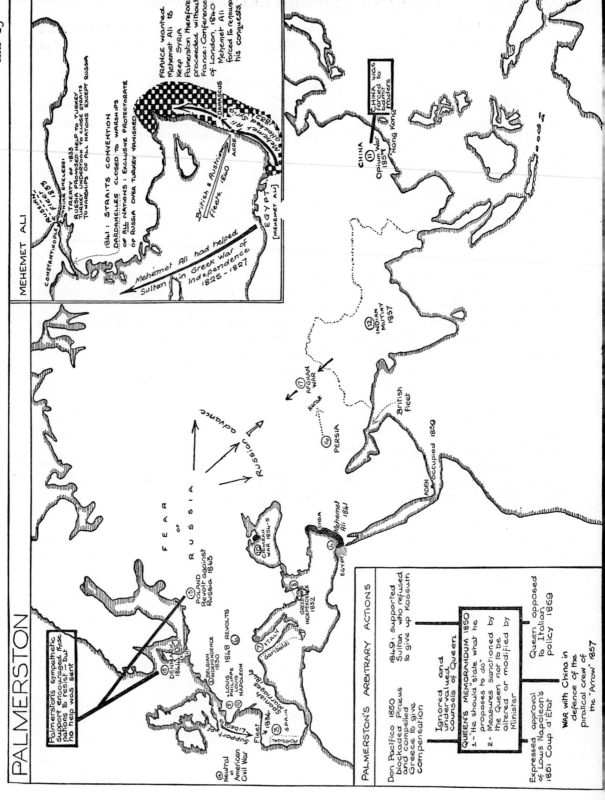

PALMERSTON

MEHEMET ALI

Palmerston's sympathetic support encouraged those nations to resist — but no help was sent

Mehemet Ali had helped Sultan in Greek War of Independence 1825-1827

CONSTANTINOPLE
RUSSIAN FLEET 1833
UNKIAR SKELESSI
DAMASCUS
Mehemet Ali occupied Syria 1833
British & Austrian fleets 1840
ACRE
EGYPT [MEHEMET ALI]

1833: TREATY of 1833 RUSSIA PROMISED HELP TO TURKEY TURKEY UNDERTOOK TO CLOSE STRAITS TO WARSHIPS OF ALL NATIONS EXCEPT RUSSIA

1841: STRAITS CONVENTION DARDANELLES CLOSED TO WARSHIPS OF ALL NATIONS: EXCLUSIVE PROTECTORATE OF RUSSIA OVER TURKEY VANISHED

FRANCE wanted Mehemet Ali to keep Syria Palmerston therefore proceeded without France: Conference of London, 1840 Mehemet Ali forced to renounce his conquests.

FEAR of RUSSIA

RUSSIAN advance

(13) POLAND revolt against Russia 1863

(15) DENMARK 1864

(8) BELGIAN INDEPENDENCE 1850

1848 REVOLTS (6)

(5) LOUIS PHILIPPE 1850
(4) LOUIS NAPOLEON

(7) ITALY Garibaldi

(9) GREEK INDEPENDENCE 1852

Liberal Support for Spanish Marriages Fleet 1834

(10) SPAIN

PORTUGAL

(14) Neutral in American Civil War

CRIMEAN WAR 1854-5 (3)

SYRIA
Mehemet Ali 1841
EGYPT

ADEN occupied 1839

British Fleet

(16) PERSIA
Herat
(17) AFGHAN WAR

(12) INDIAN MUTINY 1857

CHINA (11)
Opium War 1857
Hong Kong

CHINA WAS FORCED TO ADMIT TRADERS

PALMERSTON'S ARBITRARY ACTIONS

Don Pacifico 1850 blockaded Piraeus and compelled Greece to give compensation

1849: supported Sultan who refused to give up Kossuth

QUEEN'S MEMORANDUM 1850
1 — "He should state what he proposes to do"
2 — Measures sanctioned by the Queen not to be altered or modified by Minister

Queen opposed to Italian policy 1859

Expressed approval of Louis Napoleon's 1851 Coup d'État

Ignored and undervalued counsels of Queen

WAR with China in defence of the piratical crew of the "Arrow" 1857

PALMERSTON

FROM 1830 to 1865 Palmerston was principally responsible for British foreign policy. He was one of the outstanding figures in European diplomacy. Until the last few years of his *régime* he could safely throw the full weight of Britain's influence into European issues, and he did so in a high-handed fashion which made him unpopular abroad. His carefully considered bluff, however, had the result of increasing Britain's prestige on the Continent.

A. His Conception of the Rôle of Great Britain

In his day the British Parliamentary system was the model sought by European peoples who were striving to achieve the national unity and freedom enjoyed in this country. With the confidence in British institutions common among his contemporaries, he threw his influence on the side of liberalism, supporting national movements against inefficient and unsympathetic Governments.

But an equally strong motive was to maintain the balance of power in Europe, and he judged each new upheaval from this standpoint. He had little sympathy with a state struggling for independence if its freedom was likely to weaken the relative strength of a Great Power.

B. Attitude towards Russia

To Palmerston the Russian menace was the great shadow across Europe. He opposed the ambitions of Russia in the Balkans, fearing that further expansion would disturb the balance of power, and in the Middle East because he believed that Russia aimed at controlling India. He feared that if the Turkish Empire were overthrown Russia would threaten British trade in the Mediterranean.

C. Attitude towards France

He realized the importance of friendship with France, and to this end he co-operated with the moderate section of French opinion. But he was equally anxious to oppose the extension of French influence in Europe. He maintained the balance of power against France by his support of Belgian and Italian independence and his opposition to French influence in the Peninsula.

D. Key to Numbers on Map

(1) *Support of nationality: Belgium.* In 1830 the Belgians had overthrown the rule of the Dutch King. When Palmerston took office William I was preparing to subdue them by force, and the autocratic powers (Russia and Austria) were supporting him. The Belgians looked to France for help, and Palmerston preserved the freedom of the Belgians by co-operation with France, though he opposed the French choice of

candidate for the Belgian throne. In 1839 he strengthened the new kingdom by obtaining the recognition of Belgian neutrality by all the Powers (the Treaty of London, 1839). This was probably Palmerston's greatest diplomatic success.

(2) *Support of nationality : Greece.* Palmerston upheld the complete independence of the Greeks, and by the Treaty of 1839 an extension of the Greek boundary was obtained.

(3) *Support of nationality : Spain and Portugal.* The Carlist Party in Spain and the Miguelists in Portugal sought to overthrow liberal institutions. Palmerston made an alliance with the two Governments to which France adhered (Quadruple Alliance, 1834), promising support to the two countries in the Peninsula against the interference of the autocratic Powers (Russia, Prussia, and Austria).

(4) *Opposition to Russia : Mehemet Ali.* Palmerston was alarmed in 1833 when Turkey sought Russian help to withstand Mehemet Ali of Egypt, who had attacked Syria. By the Treaty of Unkiar Skelessi, Russia became the protector of Turkey and gained control of the Straits. Palmerston determined to oppose Russia at the first opportunity, which came in 1839, when the quarrel between the Sultan and his vassal was renewed. By this time Russia was anxious to check Mehemet Ali, who was supported by France.

Palmerston allied with Russia to force Mehemet Ali out of Syria without the knowledge of France. This weakened the friendly relations between England and France. By the Treaty of the Straits (1841) it was agreed to prohibit foreign warships from entering the Black Sea. Turkey was once more upheld, and Russian ambitions were checked—a diplomatic triumph for Palmerston.

(5) *Relations with France : Spanish marriages.* In 1830 Palmerston had built up a good understanding with France, but it was difficult to maintain owing to his high-handed diplomacy. Friction arose over Mehemet Ali and again in 1846, when Palmerston resisted Louis Philippe's attempt to gain increased influence in Spain by a suggested marriage-alliance.

(6) *Attitude to revolution : 1848.* During the year of revolution Palmerston's chief aim was to prevent a European war. He feared that France, the main support of revolution, and Russia, of absolutism, would come into conflict. He kept on good terms with both to hold them in check. He used his moral influence on behalf of freedom, but gave no practical help. In Italy he encouraged the princes to make reforms, but discouraged the French and Sardinians from leading an Italian revolt against Austria, thus delaying the triumph of Italian independence. He approved of Russia's support of Austria to put down the rising in Hungary because of the need of a strong Austrian Empire to restrain the ambitions of Russia.

(7) *Support of nationality : Italy.* As Prime Minister (1859–1865) Palmerston helped Italian independence. Without England's declaration that the Italians should be allowed to settle their own affairs, the hostility of the other Powers would have defeated Cavour when he attacked the Papal states. Britain's support enabled Garibaldi to unite Southern Italy to the North unchecked by foreign intervention.

(8) *Maintenance of national prestige : Don Pacifico.* This incident illustrates Palmerston's aggressive maintenance of British 'rights.' Don Pacifico was a British subject whose property had been damaged in a riot in Athens. Palmerston supported his excessive claims against the Greek Government with an aggressive determination

that brought censure from Parliament. But Palmerston scored a great triumph in a speech in 1852, in which he drew attention to Britain's overwhelming power to protect even the most insignificant of her subjects.

(9) *Relations with France: Napoleon III.* In 1851 Palmerston expressed his approval of Louis Napoleon's *coup d'état*, recognizing his Government as the most likely to preserve order. Nevertheless, he was always mistrustful of Napoleon III.

(10) *Opposition to Russia: Crimean War.* See map and notes on pp. 49–51.

(11) *Maintenance of national prestige and trade interests: China.* Palmerston abused the power of Britain by compelling the Chinese in 1840 to open their Empire to the trade of the West. At the end of the war Britain seized Hong Kong.

In 1857 he supported the British agent in China, who demanded the release of a native crew charged with piracy who had been seized from H.M.S. *Arrow.* A naval force was sent to Canton, and the Chinese were compelled to submit.

(12) *Security of India.* Palmerston was in office at the outbreak of the Indian Mutiny.

(13) *Support of nationality: Poland.* British public opinion was sympathetic to the Poles in their struggle for freedom from Russia. Palmerston remonstrated with Russia but took no further action. His encouragement had led the Poles to expect foreign aid. Without it their cause was hopeless.

(14) *The American Civil War: neutrality.* Palmerston maintained a policy of strict neutrality in the American Civil War. Some trouble arose with the Federal Government over the *Trent,* a British vessel on which two Southern Confederate Commissioners were sailing. War was averted largely by the influence of the Prince Consort.

(15) *Support of nationality: Schleswig and Holstein.* The Danes also suffered from the false hopes which Palmerston inspired. His outspoken threat to any Government which attacked Denmark caused the Danes to resist the attack of the German Powers in 1863, but Palmerston had no intention of keeping his word.

(16) *Security of India: Persia.* Russia incited Persia to push eastward into Afghanistan, and in 1856 the Indian Government went to war, forcing Persia to renounce a claim to any part of Afghanistan.

(17) *Security of India: Afghanistan.* The first Afghan War took place while Palmerston was Foreign Minister. He upheld Lord Auckland's policy of checking Russia's growing influence in Afghanistan. After some minor successes the British were forced to retreat.

MAP 16

DISRAELI

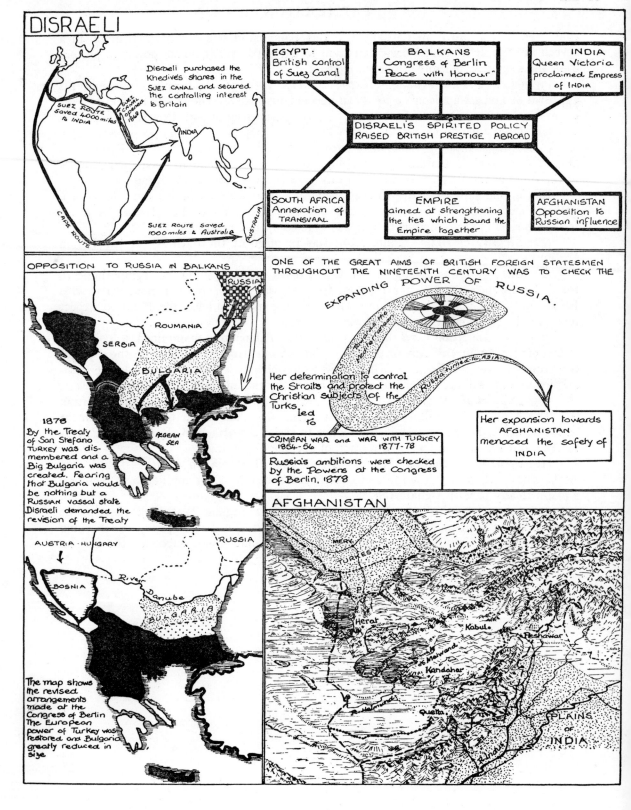

Disraeli purchased the Khedive's shares in the SUEZ CANAL and secured the controlling interest to Britain

SUEZ ROUTE Saved 4,000 miles to INDIA

SUEZ CANAL opened 1869

INDIA

CAPE ROUTE

SUEZ ROUTE saved 1000 miles to Australia

AUSTRALIA

EGYPT: British control of Suez Canal

BALKANS Congress of Berlin "Peace with Honour"

INDIA Queen Victoria proclaimed Empress of INDIA

DISRAELI'S SPIRITED POLICY RAISED BRITISH PRESTIGE ABROAD

SOUTH AFRICA Annexation of TRANSVAAL

EMPIRE aimed at strengthening the ties which bound the Empire together

AFGHANISTAN Opposition to Russian influence

OPPOSITION TO RUSSIA IN BALKANS

RUSSIA

ROUMANIA

SERBIA

BULGARIA

AEGEAN SEA

1878 By the Treaty of San Stefano TURKEY was dismembered and a Big Bulgaria was created. Fearing that Bulgaria would be nothing but a RUSSIAN vassal state Disraeli demanded the revision of the Treaty

AUSTRIA-HUNGARY

RUSSIA

BOSNIA

River Danube

BULGARIA

The map shows the revised arrangements made at the Congress of Berlin. The European power of Turkey was restored and Bulgaria greatly reduced in size

ONE OF THE GREAT AIMS OF BRITISH FOREIGN STATESMEN THROUGHOUT THE NINETEENTH CENTURY WAS TO CHECK THE

EXPANDING POWER OF RUSSIA.

Towards the Mediterranean

Russia turned to ASIA

Her determination to control the Straits and protect the Christian subjects of the Turks led to

CRIMEAN WAR and WAR WITH TURKEY 1854-56   1877-78

Russia's ambitions were checked by the Powers at the Congress of Berlin, 1878

Her expansion towards AFGHANISTAN menaced the safety of INDIA

AFGHANISTAN

MERV

TURKESTAN

Herat

Kabul

Peshawar

Meiwand

Kandahar

Quetta

Indus

PLAINS of INDIA

DISRAELI'S FOREIGN AND IMPERIAL POLICY

THESE maps illustrate the chief questions that engaged the attention of Disraeli in foreign and imperial affairs.

A. HIS POLICY

(1) Disraeli believed that the chief aim of Britain's foreign policy should be the furtherance of British imperial interests. He thought of Britain less as a European than a world power, and his imagination was kindled by the vision of a vast British Empire in the East. The strengthening of British power in India was therefore his main concern; he was anxious to safeguard Britain's communications with it. Inevitably he came into conflict with Russia.

(2) To uphold our national prestige (" Zeal for the greatness of England was the passion of his life ") he determined that Great Britain should play a prominent part in European affairs. When in opposition he attacked Gladstone's 'weak' foreign policy; when in power he placed Britain in the forefront of world politics and revived her prestige by establishing her right to share in the settlement of international disputes.

(3) Hitherto British statesmen had lacked a real interest in colonies. Disraeli made colonial expansion a deliberate policy, thus beginning a new tradition in our imperial history.

B. EGYPT

Until the opening of the Suez Canal in 1869 France had exercised most influence in Egypt, but the canal made it a link in the chain of communications with India, and British statesmen acquired a special interest in the country. In 1875 Disraeli, with great foresight, took advantage of the Khedive Ismail's bankruptcy to purchase his shares in the Suez Canal Company. This action committed Great Britain to intervention with France (Dual Control) in Egyptian affairs for the protection of her financial interests.

C. INDIA AND AFGHANISTAN

At Disraeli's suggestion the Queen adopted the title of Empress of India in 1877. He realized that this would have great significance to the oriental mind and that the dignity of the position would secure respect and loyalty from the Eastern princes.

Suspicious of Russian intrigues in Afghanistan, he sent a British agent to Kabul. Unhappily he was murdered, and to restore British prestige, Disraeli dispatched an army under Lord Roberts. The intervention proved costly and futile, and when Gladstone came into office it was withdrawn.

D. SOUTH AFRICA

A forward policy in South Africa led to further disaster. In 1877 the Transvaal was annexed. A series of disputes with the Zulus led to war, in which a small British force was overwhelmed. A subsequent victory at Ulundi did not quieten misgivings at home as to the wisdom of Disraeli's aggressive policy. (See p. 113.)

E. THE EASTERN QUESTION

Disraeli secured his most spectacular triumph in his handling of the European crisis of 1875–1878, which arose out of the Eastern question.

The growing demand of the Christian peoples of the Turkish Empire for independence and the failure of the Sultan to adopt reforms led to rebellions in Bosnia and Herzegovina in 1875. The Powers, acting in concert, wished to put pressure on the Sultan ; but Disraeli declined to act with them, fearing that intervention would weaken Turkey, whose empire he wished to preserve intact as a barrier against Russia.

The insurrection spread to Bulgaria, Serbia, and Montenegro. The inhuman cruelty of the Turks, who massacred the Bulgarian peasants, horrified the British public. Gladstone, then in opposition, called for war against the Turks, but Disraeli refused to act.

When the Powers failed to settle the problem satisfactorily, Russia acted independently. She declared war on Turkey in 1877 and, after a check at Plevna, advanced to Constantinople. Disraeli's determination to oppose Russia's entry into the Turkish capital by war if necessary caused Russia to make peace at San Stefano (refer to map). To Disraeli the terms of this settlement seemed to give Russia supreme influence in the Balkans. He demanded a revision of the treaty at a congress of the Powers. His firm stand forced Russia to agree.

The Congress of Berlin (1878). At this congress Disraeli attained his end—the destruction of the Treaty of San Stefano—without the cost of a war. The second map shows the rearrangement of territory which was agreed upon. At the same time Cyprus was added to the British Empire. Disraeli returned from Berlin claiming that he brought ' peace with honour,' and this was the general opinion of the British public. He had successfully frustrated Russia and delayed the collapse of the Turkish Empire in Europe ; but his victory was gained at the expense of the struggling nations in the Balkans, and the wisdom of his policy is open to doubt.

GLADSTONE'S FOREIGN AND COLONIAL POLICY

A. Gladstone's Approach to Foreign Affairs

(1) Gladstone's main interests were in financial and administrative reform, not in foreign affairs. His chief concern was the maintenance of peace by active co-operation with other Powers.

(2) Under Canning and Palmerston Great Britain had played a very active part in European politics—often by bluff. In his last years Palmerston discovered that his old methods would no longer work. A new era was beginning in the 'sixties of great continental armies, and Bismarck, for one, realized that Britain could not enforce any threats to interfere in Europe. The growth of railways had greatly increased the power of the countries of Central Europe. Gladstone considered that peace and isolation were more beneficial to England and to her prosperity than futile gestures of war.

(3) To this policy of non-intervention Gladstone made one striking exception. An idealist and a Christian, he believed that it was the duty of a great nation to interfere in the cause of humanity whenever foreign rulers showed inhuman cruelty. For this reason he sought to relieve the Christian peoples of the Balkans from Turkish oppression, thus challenging one of the outstanding principles of British foreign policy —the maintenance of the integrity of the Turkish Empire.

The maps help to illustrate some of the foreign and imperial problems which Gladstone's Governments helped to solve.

B. First Ministry (1868–1874)

(1) *Neutrality during the Franco-Prussian War.*
(a) Heedless of public opinion, he determined that Britain should be neutral.
(b) He sought to maintain British security by extracting a promise from both sides that neither would invade Belgium.
(c) He announced that Britain would declare war on the state which violated Belgian neutrality.

(2) *Russia.* The Czar took advantage of the European crisis during the Franco-Prussian War to denounce the restrictions imposed by the Treaty of Paris of 1856 (after the Crimean War) against Russian warships in the Black Sea.

(3) *The 'Alabama' question.* Though England was neutral during the American Civil War of 1861–1865, the Confederate cruiser *Alabama* had been allowed to escape from Birkenhead to prey upon the commerce of the Federal Government. After the war was over the U.S.A. claimed compensation for the damage done.

Gladstone submitted the claims to an International Court of Arbitration at Geneva (the first example of arbitration recorded in history) and paid the award the court made.

MAP 17

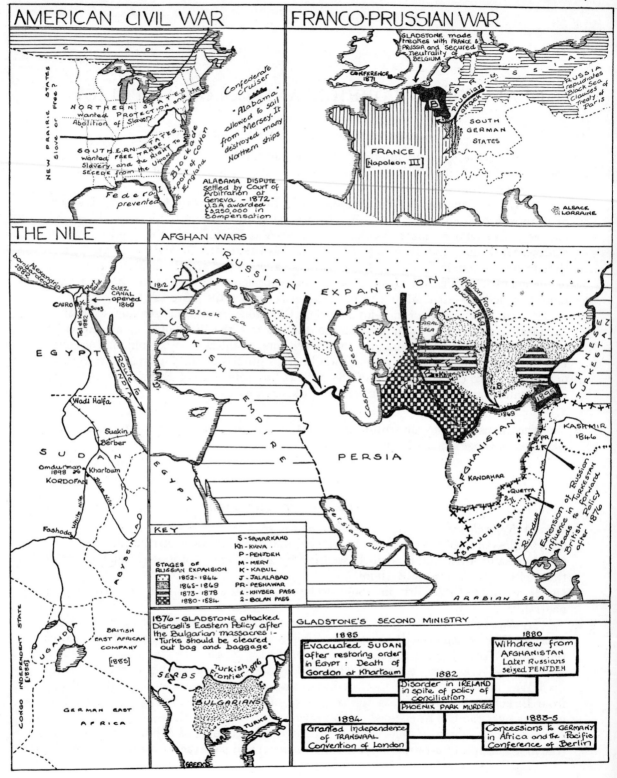

Gladstone's solution of these three problems was wise and statesmanlike. Nevertheless, many people considered that he had failed to maintain the national honour.

C. Gladstone in Opposition during Disraeli's Ministry (1874–1880)

(1) He protested against Disraeli's aggressive policy in Afghanistan, Egypt, and South Africa.

(2) He condemned the atrocities of the Turks in Bulgaria and urged the reversal of our traditional policy of protecting the Turkish Empire.

D. Second Ministry (1880–1885)

(1) *Egypt and the Suez Canal.* Disraeli's purchase of the Suez Canal shares in 1875 was Britain's first step towards the control of Egypt. Gladstone had objected to the purchase, fearing that it would later entail a military occupation to protect our financial interests. In 1881 anti-foreign riots broke out, and Gladstone unwillingly despatched an army to restore order. (Wolseley's victory at Tel el Kebir, 1882.)

(2) *The Sudan.* Gladstone had accepted responsibility for maintaining order in Egypt, but he refused to be responsible for its dependency, the Egyptian Sudan, which was disturbed by a religious fanatic, the Mahdi. In 1884 he despatched ' Chinese ' Gordon to withdraw the Egyptian forces and officials. Gordon decided that it was his duty to tame the Mahdi, and so he stayed at Khartoum. Gladstone delayed sending an army to rescue him until it was too late. The news of the fall of Khartoum and the murder of Gordon provoked violent passions against Gladstone.[1]

(3) *Russia.* Disraeli had been active in resisting Russian aggression in Afghanistan and advancing British influence. Gladstone reversed his ' forward ' policy and withdrew the English army. The Russian advance to Merv and their defeat of the Afghan army at Penjdeh in 1885 provoked British public opinion, but Gladstone refused to give way to the clamour for war against Russia.

(4) *South Africa.* Gladstone had condemned Disraeli's annexation of the Transvaal in 1877. He delayed the restoration of independence, and in 1881 the Boers attacked and defeated British forces at Majuba Hill. Instead of dispatching a large army to subdue the Boers Gladstone gave them independence (Convention of London, 1884).

(5) *Colonial claims of Germany.* Gladstone's Government gave way to Bismarck's claims to territory in the Pacific and Africa.

Gladstone's solution of these problems in a spirit alien to the temper of his age aroused hostile criticism ; he was considered ' weak ' in foreign affairs.

[1] The reconquest of the Sudan was undertaken by Salisbury in 1896, and was effected after Kitchener's victory at Omdurman in 1898.

MAP 18

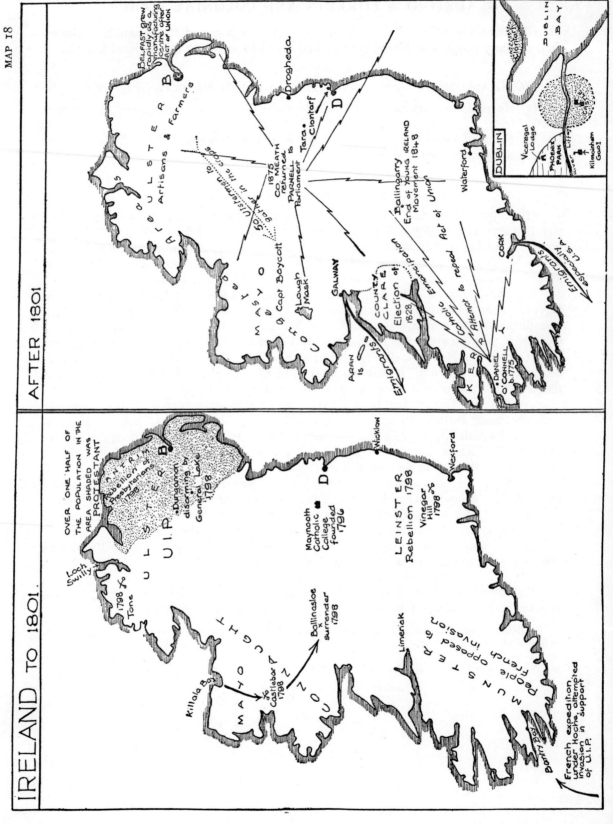

IRELAND TO 1801.

AFTER 1801

IRELAND TO 1801 (left panel):

OVER ONE HALF OF THE POPULATION IN THE AREA SHADED WAS PROTESTANT

Loch Swilly

1798 ✕ Tone

Killala B.

M A Y O

Castlebar ✕ 1798

C O N N A U G H T

Ballinasloe ✕ surrender 1798

ANTRIM Rebellion of Presbyterians 1798

U L S T E R B

•Dungannon disarming by General Lake 1798

Maynooth Catholic College founded 1796

D

Wicklow

LEINSTER Rebellion 1798

Vinegar Hill 1798 ✕

Wexford

Limerick

M U N S T E R people opposed French invasion

French expedition under Hoche, attempted invasion in support of U.I.P.

Bantry Bay

AFTER 1801 (right panel):

BELFAST grew rapidly as a manufacturing centre after Act of Union

U L S T E R B

Artisans & Farmers

Drogheda

Tara • Clontarf D

Ulstermen to the cross

50 years of rebellion

1875 CO MEATH returned PARNELL to Parliament

M A Y O

○ Capt Boycott

Lough Mask

C O N N

GALWAY

ARAN Is

COUNTY CLARE Election of 1828

Emigrants U.S.A.

K E R R Y

Catholic Emancipation

Attempt to repeal Act of Union

Ballingarry End of YOUNG IRELAND Movement 1848

Waterford

CORK

Emigrants U.S.A. especially

• DANIEL O'CONNELL b.1775

DUBLIN inset:

DUBLIN BAY

Vice-regal Lodge

PHOENIX PARK

Kilmainham Gaol

river Liffey

IRELAND (1783–1914)

ENGLAND has been less successful in her dealings with Ireland than with any other country. Treated unjustly for centuries, the Irish have regarded the English with hatred and suspicion. Foreign enemies have not failed to make use of the dangerous discontent in a country whose position is so advantageous for an attack on Britain. The fact that the safety of Britain is endangered by Ireland's disloyalty has complicated the problem of the relation between the two countries.

A. THE UNREST OF THE EIGHTEENTH CENTURY

During the eighteenth century Ireland was in a state of acute misery. (Refer also to Map 2 and notes on pp. 17–18.)

Unjust laws penalized the Catholics, and commercial prosperity was impossible owing to the restrictions on Irish trade. In 1782 the Irish had received a separate Parliament, which mitigated the harshness of many laws, but conditions were still unsatisfactory.

There were three main difficulties :

(1) *The land-problem.* The chief cause of the misery of the Irish was connected with the land. Three-quarters of Ireland was owned by English Protestant landlords ; the work was done by Irish Catholic peasants. Land was sublet into small holdings, to the profit of the landlord and the middleman. The peasants paid exorbitant rents as the population increased rapidly, and there was fierce competition for the small holdings. These small farmers lived on the verge of starvation. When a bad harvest made it impossible for them to pay their rent, they were evicted from their holdings without receiving compensation for any improvements they had made to the farm. (Refer also to notes on pp. 17–18.)

(2) *The religious problem.* The Catholics were forced to pay tithes to the English Church ; many of them were too poor to pay dues to their own Church. In Ulster there were large numbers of Presbyterians, who, though Protestants, were with the Catholics excluded from a share in the Government.

(3) *The problem of government*

(a) The Irish Parliament did not represent the nation. Only Protestants were allowed to vote and sit in Parliament, and even so, representation was limited to a group of landowners who had control of rotten boroughs. By a system of bribery the British Government still retained its influence, though the Irish Parliament was nominally free.

(b) The chief ministers of Ireland were appointed by the British Government. The Irish Parliament had little control over them.

B. THE FRENCH REVOLUTION AND THE IRISH REBELLION (1798)

The French Revolution had important effects in Ireland :

(1) It encouraged the demand for a reform of Parliament. This was advocated by Henry Grattan.

(2) It led to the growth of a revolutionary party which aimed at securing complete independence from England. For this purpose Wolfe Tone in 1791 formed a society called " The United Irishmen," the members of which were at first drawn from both Protestants and Roman Catholics. Pitt's unwillingness to grant complete freedom to the Catholics—though he had conceded the right to vote in 1793—led Wolfe Tone to seek the help of the French. A promise to abolish the tithe payments attracted the support of the peasants. The Ulster Protestants were frightened away from the movement by the violence of the Catholics.

(3) The spread of disorder and attacks on property led the Protestants of Ulster in self-defence to organize the " Orange Society " (1795).

(4) Two French attempts to invade Ireland (1796–1797) decided the Government to disarm Ulster. English armies began to punish the Irish who had assisted the French. The hatred of the Protestant soldiers let loose the religious passions of the country ; their cruelty precipitated a rebellion organized by the United Irishmen (1798). The rebellion was not formidable except in Leinster. The French troops arrived too late. (See map.)

(5) *Results of the Rebellion*

(*a*) It left a heritage of bitterness between Southern (Catholic) Ireland and Protestant Ulster.

(*b*) Pitt decided to unite the Parliaments of England and Ireland. As a solution of the religious problem, he promised Catholic emancipation, thus making union tolerable to the Catholics. Grattan and his friends opposed the loss of Irish independence. The Act of Union (1801) was only carried through the Irish Parliament by bribery on a large scale.

(*c*) The Act gave Ireland much better representation in the British Parliament than was enjoyed by either Scotland or Wales ; it provided free trade with England and the colonial empire, which improved the economic position of the country. Pitt was unable, however, to carry out his promise to give the Catholics political rights ; they had sacrificed their independence but gained no redress. The experiment of uniting the two Parliaments was doomed to be unsatisfactory.

C. IRELAND AFTER 1801

After 1801 the three problems of land, religion, and government still remained to be solved. The demand for self-government now took the form of agitation for the repeal of the Act of Union. Throughout the century Ireland was disturbed by agrarian outrages and political agitations.

(1) *Daniel O'Connell.* O'Connell—' the liberator '—a moderate reformer, who opposed violence, led the struggle for Catholic emancipation. He formed an association in 1823, collecting a ' rent ' from the peasants ; he fought elections and was himself

elected for County Clare in 1828. Fearing civil war, the British Government agreed to his demands.

By the Catholic Emancipation Act of 1829 Catholics were eligible for all but the highest offices of state.

For a time O'Connell united with the Whig party and supported the union, but, discouraged by their limited reforms, in 1840 he formed a " Repeal Association." Vigorous agitation throughout Ireland culminated in the organization of a monster demonstration at Clontarf, near Dublin, in 1843. This meeting was prohibited by Peel. Hitherto O'Connell had restrained the more advanced section of young Irishmen, who advocated rebellion, but his failure to hold the Clontarf meeting discredited him. " Young Ireland " grew more powerful.

(2) *The Irish famine and its effects.* In 1845 and the following years a blight attacked the potato crop, which was the principal food for the Irish peasants. Private charity, relief works, emigration, and even the repeal of the Corn Laws did not save thousands of the peasants from starvation. The effects of the famine were :

(*a*) From this time the population of Ireland steadily decreased. Irishmen emigrated to England and America. They carried their hatred and bitterness to their new homes. The Fenian Movement began in America.

(*b*) Disputes between landlords and tenants became increasingly violent. Peasants were evicted because they could not pay their rents ; landlords united holdings as large farms were more profitable. Persistent attacks on property disturbed the peace.

(*c*) Discontent strengthened the " Young Ireland " movement. A rebellion, organized by Smith O'Brien in 1848, was a failure.

(3) *The Fenians.* Founded in 1858 in America, the society aimed at establishing an independent republic in Ireland. The Fenians were active in 1866–1867, planning an attack on Canada and disorder in Ireland and England. Their efforts at direct action failed, but they aroused the attention of the British public to the grievances of Ireland. Gladstone was impressed. (" My mission is to pacify Ireland.")

(4) *Gladstone's work.* During his first ministry

(*a*) he disestablished the Irish Church and

(*b*) he passed a Land Act which secured a tenant in his holding if he paid his rent— an insufficient remedy, however, because the rents were too high.

(5) *Charles Stewart Parnell—' the uncrowned king of Ireland.'* Parnell, a Protestant landowner, formed a well-disciplined party in Parliament pledged to secure the independence of Ireland. He had financial support from American sympathizers.

(*a*) As president of the Land League (founded 1879) he resisted the exactions of the landlords by a ' no rent ' campaign. Opposed to violence, he advocated a policy of ' boycott.'

(*b*) In Parliament he and his followers adopted a policy of obstruction ; they delayed all business until the Government dealt with Irish grievances.

The 1881 Land Act passed by Gladstone was Parnell's triumph. Rents were reduced by twenty per cent., but the peasants were not satisfied.

Crime and murder (*e.g.*, Phœnix Park Murders) forced the Government to adopt harsh measures, but Gladstone, convinced of the justice of the Irish demand for independence, was not turned aside from his purpose of granting it. He twice attempted to pass a Home Rule Bill (1886 and 1893), but without success. The

E

Protestants of Ulster were strongly opposed, and the English nation was not yet converted to the idea.

(6) *After Parnell*. The Conservative Party, which was in power from 1885 to 1892, and 1894 to 1902, attempted to kill the demand for Home Rule by a policy of ' firmness and kindness.'

(*a*) They put down disorder with a heavy hand.

(*b*) They introduced Land Purchase Acts, advancing money to enable tenants to purchase their lands.

(*c*) They introduced relief measures for the distress in the congested areas of the West.

Increased prosperity came to Ireland, but the desire for self-government still remained. Its latest form, the Sinn Fein Movement, took shape in 1905. Its aim was the complete independence of the Irish. At the same time opposition to Home Rule grew fiercer in Ulster.

In 1912 the Liberal Party, under Asquith, introduced a third Home Rule Bill. In spite of a rebellion in Ulster the Bill was passed in July, 1914. As the Great War broke out the operation of the measure was postponed.

EUROPE IN 1914: THE ARMED CAMPS

THIS map emphasizes:

(1) One of the chief causes of the Great War—the existence of two groups of alliances of opposing powers.

(2) Britain's reasons for joining one of these alliances.

A. THE TRIPLE ALLIANCE

Bismarck formed the Triple Alliance to ensure the safety of Germany against the revengeful attitude of France after the Franco-Prussian War of 1870. He had failed to maintain an alliance of the three autocratic powers—Prussia, Austria, and Russia —owing to the divergent interests of Austria and Russia in the Balkans. The Dual Alliance between Austria and Prussia of 1879 provided for mutual defence in case of attack from Russia.

Italy, on the initiative of Bismarck, became a partner in this defensive pact in 1882, largely because France had seized Tunis.

B. THE TRIPLE ENTENTE

(1) *Franco-Russian agreement.* Bismarck had made an effort to retain friendship with Russia, but after his dismissal by the Emperor William II, Russia drew apart from Germany. Both France and Russia felt the need of co-operation, and a military convention for defensive purposes was concluded in 1894.

(2) *Britain's 'splendid isolation.'* At this period Great Britain, the colonial rival of France in Africa and Asia and the suspicious opponent of Russian expansion, was unfriendly to both of these Powers. Her statesmen were unwilling to make allies.

(3) *Anglo-French entente* (1904). Two factors brought about the 'Entente Cordiale' between England and France.

(a) *Anglo-German rivalry* made Britain realize the disadvantage of 'splendid isolation.' German hostility was shown in the rapid growth of her navy, increasing friction in the colonies, and commercial competition.

(b) *Russo-Japanese enmity* lessened the value to France of the Russian alliance.

France and Britain settled their outstanding differences all over the world. Most important of these agreements were France's recognition of British control of Egypt and Britain's agreement to French expansion in Morocco.

(4) *Anglo-Russian agreement* (1907). Differences between Britain and Russia were deep-seated. Enmity had lasted a century. Only the weakness of Russia after her defeat by Japan and the fear of Britain at the growing menace of German militarism, aided by a mutual friendship with France, made the agreement possible.

Disputes over Afghanistan, Persia, and Tibet were settled in 1907.

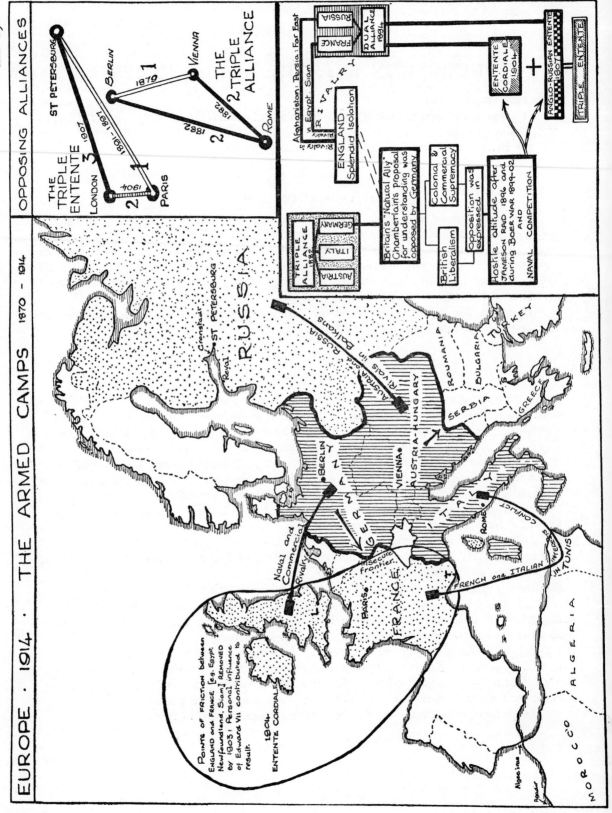

MAP 19

EUROPE · 1914 · THE ARMED CAMPS 1870 – 1914

OPPOSING ALLIANCES

THE TRIPLE ENTENTE

ST PETERSBURG

Berlin

Vienna

Rome

PARIS

LONDON

1879
1882
1881–1887
1907
1891–1907
1904

2 THE TRIPLE ALLIANCE

RUSSIA

ST PETERSBURG
Cronstadt
Reval

BERLIN
GERMANY

VIENNA
AUSTRIA-HUNGARY

ROUMANIA
SERBIA
BULGARIA
TURKEY
GREECE

ITALY
ROME

FRANCE
PARIS

SPAIN
MOROCCO
ALGERIA
TUNIS

Austria and Russia rivals in Balkans

Naval and Commercial Rivalry

Insecure frontier

FRENCH and ITALIAN NAVAL CONFLICT

Points of friction between England and France [e.g. Egypt, Newfoundland, Siam] removed by 1905; Personal influence of Edward VII contributed to result.

1904 ENTENTE CORDIALE

TRIPLE ALLIANCE 1882
GERMANY
AUSTRIA
ITALY

Rivalry in Afghanistan: Persia: Far East Rivalry in Egypt: Siam

RUSSIA
FRANCE
DUAL ALLIANCE 1894

ENTENTE CORDIALE 1904

ANGLO-RUSSIAN ENTENTE 1907

TRIPLE ENTENTE

ENGLAND Splendid Isolation

Britain's "Natural Ally" Chamberlain's proposal for understanding was opposed by Germany

Colonial & Commercial Supremacy

British Liberalism

Opposition was expressed in

Hostile attitude after Jameson Raid 1896 and during Boer War 1899-02 AND NAVAL COMPETITION

C. The Armed Camp

These two alliances helped to cause the War because :

(1) A quarrel between any two states involved the rest.

(2) A sense of insecurity led to the growth of armaments.

Crises in Morocco (1905 and 1911) and in the Balkans (1908) illustrated the imminent danger of war, which the rivalry of Russia and Austria finally precipitated.

MAP 20

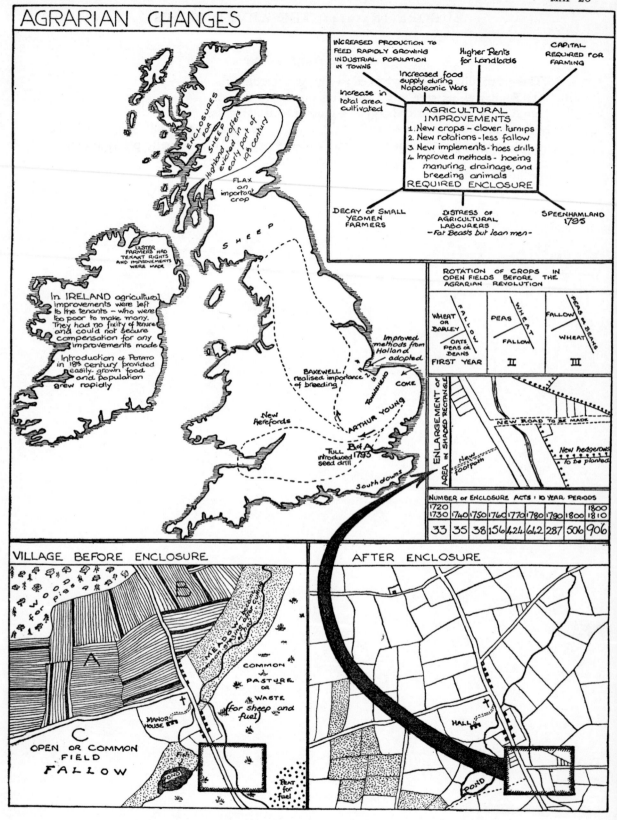

THE AGRARIAN REVOLUTION

BEFORE the great changes which occurred towards the end of the eighteenth century England was principally an agricultural country, a land of yeomen farmers working their own land as the peasants of France do to-day. Even those people who were engaged in the manufacturing-industry—*e.g.*, the hand-loom weavers—worked in the fields for part of the year.

The land was then all-important ; possession of it gave its owners not only their incomes, but their social status and political power. Compared with modern agriculture, three characteristics are striking :

(1) The agricultural communities were practically self-supporting ; they grew their own wheat, brewed their own beer, and made their own houses, clothes, and implements.

(2) The standard of farming was very low, especially in the North of England.

(3) About one half of the country was waste land.

A. CAUSES OF THE AGRARIAN CHANGES

(1) The landed gentry had acquired knowledge of improved methods of farming. Pioneers, such as Tull, Townshend, Coke, and Bakewell, had demonstrated their value ; the example of the Dutch was effective, and the propaganda work of Arthur Young spread the new ideas over the country.

(2) The increase in wealth—derived largely from the profits of commerce—provided capital to make experiments.

(3) The success of the earlier enclosures from the landowners' point of view—more profits and higher rents—stimulated the movement.

(4) The high prices obtained during the Napoleonic Wars for agricultural produce encouraged farmers to adopt methods which would increase production.

(5) The heavy import-duties on corn after 1815 had the same effect.

B. AGRARIAN CHANGES

(1) *Improvements in the technique of farming*

(a) Introduction of new machinery (*e.g.*, Tull's drill, reapers, root-cutters).
(b) New methods of drainage.
(c) New crops (*e.g.*, lucerne grass, turnips).
(d) New rotations of crops (see inset diagram).
(e) Improved methods of breeding animals.

(2) *Changes in agricultural organization which the new technique involved*

(a) *The enclosure of the open fields and common pasture.* The old communal system was wasteful and laborious because :

(i) Improvements in technique—weeding, manuring, drainage, rotation of crops, introduction of new crops or winter crops, were impossible ; a progressive farmer had to follow the conservative majority.

(ii) Common pasture of animals made it impossible to prevent the spread of disease ; it was therefore useless to try to improve the breed of sheep and cattle.

(iii) A large amount of land was wasted—in the fallow field, in the baulks between the strips, in footpaths, and in the common wastes and pastures.

(iv) The farmer's time was wasted—in moving from one of the scattered strips to another, and in unnecessary quarrels and lawsuits.

The map shows how the holdings of scattered strips were consolidated into compact farms. At the same time the common waste was also enclosed and divided.

N.B. There had been many enclosures creating compact farms before the Agrarian Revolution of the eighteenth century, especially in south-eastern England.

(b) *The creation of large farms let on long leases.* The new agricultural methods demanded larger farms and the abolition of short leases. They affected, therefore, those farmers who already had compact farms whether they were freeholders or leaseholders.

(i) The freeholder, whose holding was small, found it was not economical to use the new, more elaborate, and much more expensive machinery—even if he had the money to buy it.

(ii) The leaseholders frequently held their farms on very short leases—for terms of one or two years. Any improvements they made which resulted in greater harvests might cause the landowner to increase their rents. If evicted, tenants received no compensation for any improvements they might have made to the farms.

C. The Main Results of the Agrarian Changes

(1) *Scientific agriculture*

(a) The new methods produced more food, better food, and cheaper food. English farming became, technically, the best in the world.

(b) Without improvements in agriculture the growth of towns, with their manufacturing-industries, would have been impossible.

(c) The increased food-supply enabled Britain to support a growing population during the Napoleonic Wars.

(2) *Distress.* The enclosures benefited the big landowners, but caused much distress to the smaller yeomen farmer.

(a) There was much injustice in the redistribution of the land.

(b) The enclosure of the waste hit the poorest classes, who had no arable land but mere rights of pasture. (Note on map some of the tiny corner-patches they were awarded.) The rights of those who could not produce legal evidence of title were frequently ignored altogether.

(c) The cost of enclosure fell most hardly on the smaller men—*i.e.*, Parliamentary expenses, Commissioners' charges, fencing, and drainage-costs.

(d) The by-employments (cottage-industries, such as weaving) disappeared about the same time with the development of the factory system.

(3) *Disappearance of the free farmers.* Owing to the expense involved in the new farming the smallholders, hard pressed financially, sold their farms and either left

the countryside to become workers in the new factory towns or became landless agricultural labourers (see note below).

D. The New Organization of Agriculture

In the same way that the new inventions in industry destroyed the old domestic industries and produced a factory system, so the Agrarian Revolution broke up the village community. Agriculture, like cotton and iron, became a capitalized industry in which there were three social divisions :

(1) *Landowners.* The old landed gentry—the seventeenth-century squires—benefited most from the great changes. Many of them who had previously taken a personal interest in their villages now became absentee landlords, living in town on the increased rents they received and visiting the countryside only to hunt the fox or shoot the pheasant. Newly-rich merchants and manufacturers bought land ; seeking only social and political influence, they had little interest (beyond rent) in farming.

(2) *Tenants.* The wealthier yeomen, with adequate capital, leased large farms for long periods and introduced the new scientific methods. They were thus able to pay increased rents to the landowners.

(3) *Labourers.* The smaller yeomen formed a class of wage-earners dependent on the tenant farmer for a livelihood. Their masters, acting as Justices of the Peace, fixed their wages so low that they were compelled to seek the support of the Poor Law (refer Speenhamland, p. 83). Combinations to improve conditions were forbidden (refer Tolpuddle, p. 33). The introduction of more and more complex machinery as the nineteenth century progressed depreciated their only remaining asset—skill.

MAP 21

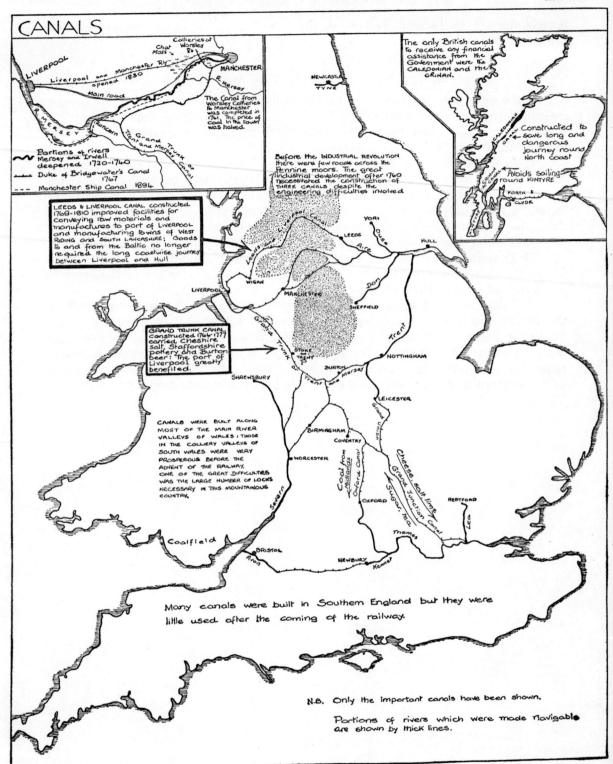

CANALS

Liverpool and Manchester Rly opened 1830

Collieries of Worsley
Chat Moss
MANCHESTER
R. Mersey
Main road
Runcorn
Grand Trunk or Trent and Mersey Canal

The Canal from Worsley Collieries to Manchester was completed in 1761. The price of Coal in the Town was halved.

~~~ Portions of rivers Mersey and Irwell deepened 1720-1740
▬▬ Duke of Bridgewater's Canal 1767
- - - Manchester Ship Canal 1894

The only British canals to receive any financial assistance from the Government were the CALEDONIAN and the CRINAN.

Constructed to save long and dangerous journey round North coast

Avoids sailing round KINTYRE

CALEDONIAN CANAL
CRINAN CANAL
FORTH & CLYDE

Before the INDUSTRIAL REVOLUTION there were few roads across the Pennine moors. The great industrial development after 1760 necessitated the construction of three canals despite the engineering difficulties involved

NEWCASTLE
TYNE

YORK
OUSE
LEEDS
Aire
HULL
Leeds and Liverpool Canal
WIGAN
LIVERPOOL
MANCHESTER
Don
SHEFFIELD
Trent

LEEDS & LIVERPOOL CANAL constructed 1769-1810 improved facilities for conveying raw materials and manufactures to port of Liverpool and manufacturing towns of West Riding and South Lancashire; Goods to and from the Baltic no longer required the long coastwise journey between Liverpool and Hull

GRAND TRUNK CANAL constructed 1766-1777 carried Cheshire salt, Staffordshire pottery and Burton beer; the port of Liverpool greatly benefited.

Grand Trunk or Trent and Mersey
STOKE on TRENT
BURTON
NOTTINGHAM
SHREWSBURY
LEICESTER

CANALS WERE BUILT ALONG MOST OF THE MAIN RIVER VALLEYS OF WALES; THOSE IN THE COLLIERY VALLEYS OF SOUTH WALES WERE VERY PROSPEROUS BEFORE THE ADVENT OF THE RAILWAY. ONE OF THE GREAT DIFFICULTIES WAS THE LARGE NUMBER OF LOCKS NECESSARY IN THIS MOUNTAINOUS COUNTRY.

BIRMINGHAM
COVENTRY
WORCESTER
Grand Union
Coal from Midlands
Oxford Canal
Cheese, salt, lime
Grand Junction Canal
OXFORD
Sugar, Tea
Severn
HERTFORD
Lea
Thames

Coalfield
BRISTOL
Avon
NEWBURY
Kennet

Many canals were built in Southern England but they were little used after the coming of the railway.

N.B. Only the important canals have been shown.

Portions of rivers which were made navigable are shown by thick lines.

CANALS

DURING the seventy years (1770–1840) when the Industrial Revolution was transforming England into the foremost manufacturing-country of the world, canals were the main arteries of inland communication.

A. THE NEED FOR CANALS

(1) Road-transport was difficult and expensive (see Map 22).

(2) River-transport was inadequate even on the sections where the river-channels had been deepened.

(3) The growing traffic of the country required increased transport-facilities ; the increasing populations of the towns required more food and more coal.

B. THE PROVISION OF CANALS

(1) The first canals were built to meet special needs : the Duke of Bridgewater built his first canal to cheapen the cost of taking coal from his Worsley collieries to Manchester ; the Grand Trunk Canal was undertaken to meet the needs of the rising industry of the North Staffordshire potteries.

(2) The financial success of the early canals and the obvious advantages to trade led to the construction of canals in all parts of the country. *N.B.* There was no scientific planning from a national point of view—and no Government assistance, except for two canals in Scotland which were not constructed for the purpose of inland trade—and this accounts for the lack of uniformity in size, depth, and distribution.

(3) The canal-system grew up with the Industrial Revolution. At first the goods carried were chiefly food, coal, lime, and stone ; later, as the new manufacturing-industries developed, the canals fed them with raw materials and distributed their finished goods.

(4) The early canal engineers, even when illiterate, like Brindley, showed that natural difficulties could be overcome by the making of tunnels and viaducts ; a new class of ' navvies ' (*i.e.*, ' navigators ') was created. The new technique was later applied to the improvement of roads and the making of railways.

C. THE EFFECTS OF THE CANALS

(1) They provided a speedier, cheaper, and more reliable transport-system for goods than the country had ever known—*e.g.*, the rate per ton for goods from Liverpool to the Potteries in 1777 was £2, 10s. by road and 13s. 4d. by canal.

(2) They enabled goods to be carried to more distant parts of the country—*e.g.*, the trade in wheat before canals was mainly local ; wheat could be carried by canal a hundred miles for 5s. a quarter.

(3) Cheaper and more efficient transport enabled the town-population to grow.

Without speedier and cheaper methods of obtaining food and raw materials the urbanization of the Industrial Revolution would have been impossible.

(4) They provided a possible transport-system for perishable and fragile articles.

(5) They stimulated the development of the ports (especially Liverpool) by enlarging the hinterlands to and from which the imports and exports came.

(6) They enabled goods to be taken across country to avoid a long coastal journey. " The Leeds and Liverpool Canal is a highway from Liverpool to the Baltic."

D. THE DECLINE OF CANALS

The canals met a real need and were amazingly successful. Although the cost of transport was generally reduced to a quarter of what it had been, the canal companies made large profits. No obstacles were too great to be overcome. By the end of the century three canals had been constructed across the Pennines.

The coming of the railway marks the end of the canal era.

(1) Improved organization would have checked their decline. The lack of uniformity in size and depth, the absence of through rates, and their unsuitability for mechanical transport are examples of defects which could have been remedied.

(2) The hilly character of Britain—necessitating frequent locks, which cause delay—remained an insuperable obstacle.

(3) Many of the canal companies opposed the Parliamentary Bills authorizing the construction of railways, and the opposition was bought out by the railway companies. Thus many of the English canals are railway-owned and, though generally a dead loss to the railway companies to the extent that compensation is being paid, are not competitors for the carriage of goods (*e.g.*, Kennet and Avon Canal was bought out by the Great Western Railway Company ; the Birmingham Canal was bought out by the London-to-Birmingham Railway—now part of the L.M.S.).

ROADS

A. BEFORE THE INDUSTRIAL REVOLUTION

(1) From the time of the Romans until the seventeenth century, rivers were more important than roads for the transport of goods and people.

(2) The roads were mere tracks, with little traffic on them ; towns, with their surrounding villages, were practically self-sufficing.

(3) The Tudors had entrusted the repair of the roads to the parishes, but the work done was unsatisfactory.

(4) The increase in wheeled traffic in the seventeenth century showed up the inadequacy of the roads—especially in the clay areas of the country. Transport, according to contemporary writers (*e.g.*, Defoe), was difficult and dangerous and very slow.

(5) *Turnpike trusts.* To keep the roads in better condition 'trusts' were instituted from 1663 onward, and authorized to levy tolls from road-users to pay for the cost of road-upkeep. The trusts were most active just before the beginning of the canal era (1760–1770). Their efficiency varied greatly.

B. AFTER THE INDUSTRIAL REVOLUTION

(1) *Improved technique in road-construction and repair.* Up to the end of the eighteenth century legislation had tried to adapt the traffic to the roads (*e.g.*, regulations regarding the width of wheels, etc.). The importance of the work of the great road-engineers—Metcalf, Telford, Macadam—is that it enabled this policy to be reversed. Roads began to be planned and constructed scientifically.

(2) The improvement of the roads made possible the development of faster passenger services. The coaching-era had its heyday in the decade 1820–1830.

(3) The coming of the railway ruined the turnpike trusts ; roads were deserted except for local traffic until the invention of the motor-car at the end of the century.

MAP 22

ROADS

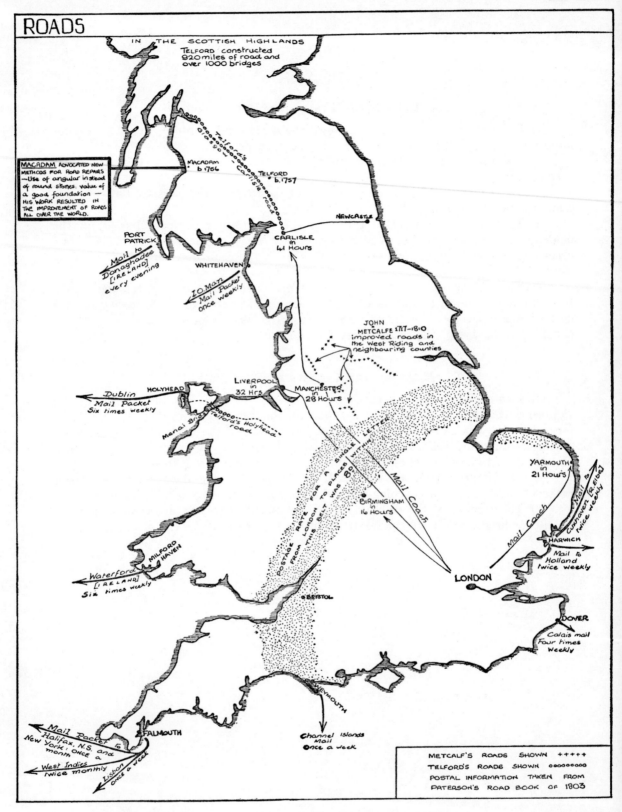

IN THE SCOTTISH HIGHLANDS Telford constructed 920 miles of road and over 1000 bridges

MACADAM ADVOCATED NEW METHODS FOR ROAD REPAIRS —Use of angular instead of round stones; value of a good foundation — HIS WORK RESULTED IN THE IMPROVEMENT OF ROADS ALL OVER THE WORLD.

MACADAM b. 1756

TELFORD b. 1757

Telford's Glasgow - Carlisle road

NEWCASTLE

CARLISLE in 41 Hours

PORT PATRICK

Mail to Donaghadee [IRELAND] every evening

WHITEHAVEN

I.O.Man Mail Packet once weekly

JOHN METCALFE 1717–1810 improved roads in the West Riding and neighbouring counties

Dublin Mail Packet Six times weekly

HOLYHEAD

Menai Br. & Telford's Holyhead road

LIVERPOOL in 32 Hrs.

MANCHESTER in 28 Hours

YARMOUTH in 21 Hours

Mail to Cuxhaven [R. side] twice weekly

Mail Coach

BIRMINGHAM in 16 Hours

Mail Coach

HARWICH

Mail to Holland twice weekly

POSTAGE RATE FOR A SINGLE LETTER FROM LONDON TO PLACES WITHIN THIS BELT WAS 8D.

Waterford [IRELAND] Six times weekly

MILFORD HAVEN

BRISTOL

LONDON

DOVER

Calais mail four times weekly

PLYMOUTH

Mail Packet to Halifax, N.S. and New York: once a month

West Indies twice monthly

Lisbon once a week

FALMOUTH

Channel Islands Mail once a week

METCALF'S ROADS SHOWN +++++
TELFORD'S ROADS SHOWN oooooooo
POSTAL INFORMATION TAKEN FROM PATERSON'S ROAD BOOK OF 1803

RAILWAYS

THE development of railways in Britain was closely connected with the coal-industry. In their evolution two stages can be noticed.

A. PROVISION OF RAILS ALONG ROADS

In the seventeenth century it had been observed that the provision of rails facilitated the pulling of moving bodies. The earliest 'railways' were simply lines of wooden blocks along which hopper wagons could be drawn more easily. Iron rails became general after 1770. The value of a flanged rail was recognized after about 1780.

B. APPLICATION OF STEAM-POWER TO LOCOMOTION

Watt's improved steam-engine (1765) came into general use after 1786, and was utilized to pull the wagons along the tramways. In 1814 George Stephenson made the first practical steam-locomotive (" Puffing Billy ").

These railways or wagon-ways were important in all the coalfields, but especially so in Durham, where canal-construction had been impossible owing to the nature of the ground. In other districts railways connected collieries and ironworks with canals or navigable rivers.

C. STOCKTON AND DARLINGTON RAILWAY

This famous railway was built in 1825 to carry coal from collieries in Co. Durham to navigable water. Its importance in the history of railways is due to its demonstration that :
(1) The steam-locomotive was superior to the horse-traction.
(2) Railways were just as suitable for passenger as for goods traffic.
(3) Unlike canal companies, which merely provided a 'permanent way,' railway companies would have to provide vehicles and means of locomotion.

D. LIVERPOOL AND MANCHESTER RAILWAY

This was important because it was :
(1) The first railway which threatened the canal and waterway interests.
(2) The first company to buy out opposition (*i.e.*, of the Bridgewater Trustees).
(3) The first real passenger railway.
(4) The line which first showed the great possibilities of the locomotive and the enormous advantages to be gained from railway-construction.

The maps show the early development of railways in Britain. Their close connexion with the coal-trade is obvious. Even in 1844 the network of lines is closest on the

MAP 23

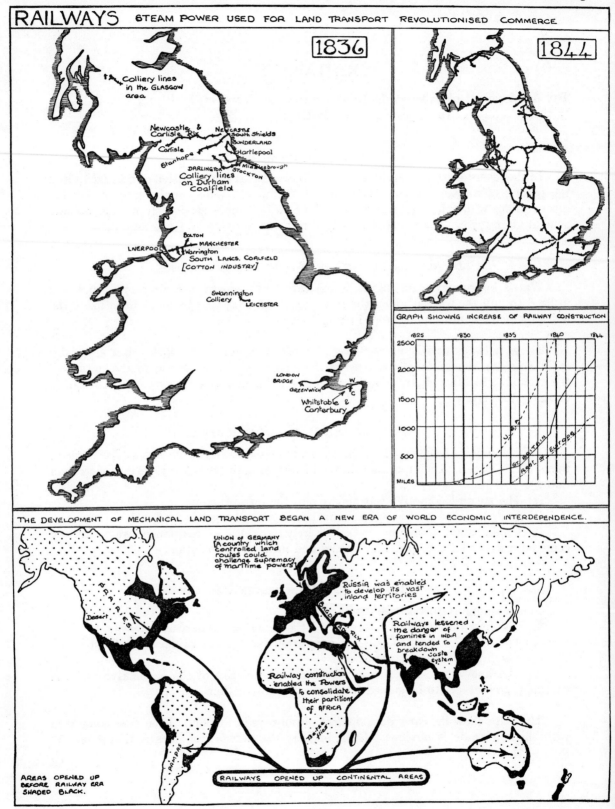

RAILWAYS
STEAM POWER USED FOR LAND TRANSPORT REVOLUTIONISED COMMERCE

1836

Colliery lines in the GLASGOW area

Newcastle & Carlisle Rly.
Newcastle
South Shields
SUNDERLAND
Carlisle
Hartlepool
Stanhope
DARLINGTON
STOCKTON
Middlesbrough
Colliery lines on Durham Coalfield

BOLTON
MANCHESTER
LIVERPOOL
Warrington
SOUTH LANCS. COALFIELD
[COTTON INDUSTRY]

Swannington Colliery
LEICESTER

LONDON BRIDGE
GREENWICH
W
C
Whitstable & Canterbury

1844

GRAPH SHOWING INCREASE OF RAILWAY CONSTRUCTION

1825 1830 1835 1840 1844
2500
2000
1500
1000
500
MILES

U.S.A.
GT. BRITAIN
REST OF EUROPE

THE DEVELOPMENT OF MECHANICAL LAND TRANSPORT BEGAN A NEW ERA OF WORLD ECONOMIC INTERDEPENDENCE.

PRAIRIES
Desert

UNION OF GERMANY [A country which controlled land routes could challenge supremacy of maritime powers]

Russia was enabled to develop its vast inland territories

Railways lessened the danger of famines in INDIA and tended to breakdown Caste system

Railway construction enabled the Powers to consolidate their partitions of AFRICA

Tsetse flies

PAMPAS

AREAS OPENED UP BEFORE RAILWAY ERA SHADED BLACK.

RAILWAYS OPENED UP CONTINENTAL AREAS

coalfields ; the other lines link together the great cities. *N.B.* An important line not shown on this map is the G.N.R., from King's Cross. It was not built until 1850 ; the district from London to Doncaster along this route is purely agricultural.

E. RAILWAYS OPENED UP THE WORLD

The railways of Britain supplemented and improved an existing system of communications. In other countries, and more especially in the great continental interiors, the building of railways was a revolution ; the railways were built first, and agriculture, industry, and population followed. The map indicates some of the important consequences of railway-construction.

MAP 24

LABOUR MOVEMENTS

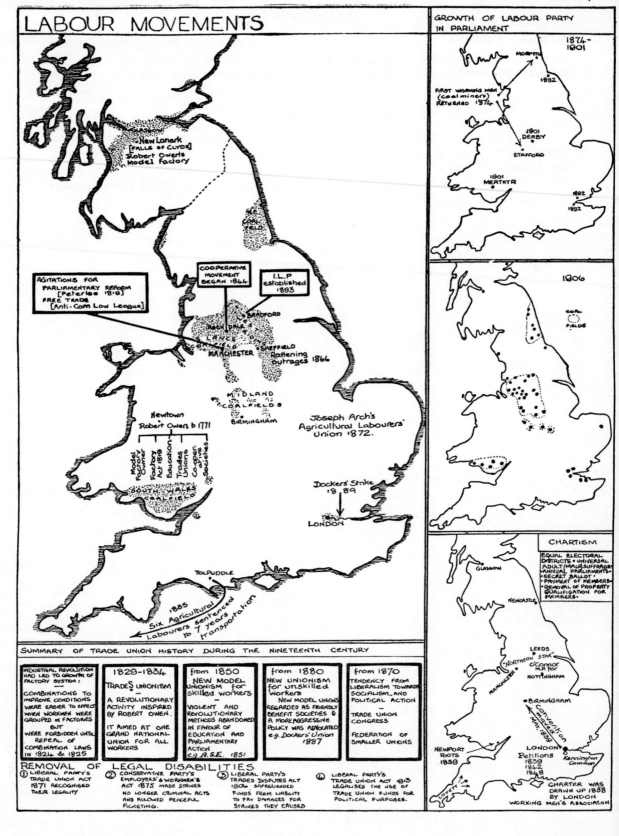

New Lanark [Falls of Clyde] Robert Owen's Model Factory

N.E. COAL FIELD

AGITATIONS FOR PARLIAMENTARY REFORM [Peterloo 1819] FREE TRADE [Anti-Corn Law League]

CO-OPERATIVE MOVEMENT BEGAN 1844

I.L.P established 1893

BRADFORD
ROCHDALE
LANCS. PITS
LEEDS
MANCHESTER
SHEFFIELD Rattening outrages 1866

MIDLAND COALFIELDS
BIRMINGHAM

Newtown Robert Owen b 1771

Model Factory Owner
Factory Act 1819
Education
Trades Unions
Co-operative Societies

SOUTH WALES COALFIELD

Joseph Arch's Agricultural Labourers' Union 1872.

Dockers' Strike 1889
London

TOLPUDDLE
1835 Six Agricultural Labourers sentenced to 7 years transportation

GROWTH OF LABOUR PARTY IN PARLIAMENT

1874–1901

MORPETH
1892
FIRST WORKING MEN (coal miners) RETURNED 1874
1901 DERBY
STAFFORD
1901 MERTHYR
1892
1892

1906

COAL FIELDS

CHARTISM

EQUAL ELECTORAL DISTRICTS · UNIVERSAL ADULT (MALE) SUFFRAGE · SECRET BALLOT · ANNUAL PARLIAMENTS · PAYMENT OF MEMBERS · REMOVAL OF PROPERTY QUALIFICATION FOR MEMBERS.

GLASGOW
NEWCASTLE
LEEDS
"NORTHERN STAR" O'Connor M.P. for NOTTINGHAM
MANCHESTER
BIRMINGHAM
Convention May 1839
NEWPORT RIOTS 1839
LONDON Petitions 1839 1842 1848 Kennington Common
LOVETT

CHARTER WAS DRAWN UP 1838 BY LONDON WORKING MEN'S ASSOCIATION

SUMMARY OF TRADE UNION HISTORY DURING THE NINETEENTH CENTURY

INDUSTRIAL REVOLUTION HAD LED TO GROWTH OF FACTORY SYSTEM:

COMBINATIONS TO IMPROVE CONDITIONS WERE EASIER TO EFFECT WHEN WORKMEN WERE GROUPED IN FACTORIES BUT WERE FORBIDDEN UNTIL REPEAL OF COMBINATION LAWS IN 1824 & 1825

1829–1834 TRADES UNIONISM – A REVOLUTIONARY ACTIVITY INSPIRED BY ROBERT OWEN. IT AIMED AT ONE GRAND NATIONAL UNION FOR ALL WORKERS

from 1850 NEW MODEL UNIONISM for skilled workers – VIOLENT AND REVOLUTIONARY METHODS ABANDONED IN FAVOUR OF EDUCATION AND PARLIAMENTARY ACTION e.g. A.S.E. 1851

from 1880 NEW UNIONISM for unskilled workers NEW MODEL UNIONS REGARDED AS FRIENDLY BENEFIT SOCIETIES & A MORE AGGRESSIVE POLICY WAS ADVOCATED e.g. Dockers' Union 1887

from 1870 TENDENCY FROM LIBERALISM TOWARDS SOCIALISM AND POLITICAL ACTION – TRADE UNION CONGRESS – FEDERATION OF SMALLER UNIONS

REMOVAL OF LEGAL DISABILITIES

① LIBERAL PARTY'S TRADE UNION ACT 1871 RECOGNISED THEIR LEGALITY

② CONSERVATIVE PARTY'S EMPLOYERS' & WORKMEN'S ACT 1875 MADE STRIKES NO LONGER CRIMINAL ACTS AND ALLOWED PEACEFUL PICKETING.

③ LIBERAL PARTY'S TRADES DISPUTES ACT 1906 SAFEGUARDED FUNDS FROM LIABILITY TO PAY DAMAGES FOR STRIKES THEY CAUSED

④ LIBERAL PARTY'S TRADE UNION ACT 1913 LEGALISED THE USE OF TRADE UNION FUNDS FOR POLITICAL PURPOSES.

LABOUR MOVEMENTS

THE early part of the nineteenth century made up the most disastrous years that the working classes of England had known. Wages were low; hours were long; conditions of labour were uncontrolled; and prices of food and clothes were increased by heavy taxation. Labour, like coal and cotton, was a commodity to be bought in the cheapest market.

During this period Radical reformers agitated for better conditions, and much of the history of labour-movements is bound up with the career of Robert Owen. Born in 1771, he became a successful cotton-manufacturer, and in his new factory town at New Lanark he introduced various reforms. He improved factory conditions and was concerned with the education of his employees and their children. He was associated with the first co-operative societies. In 1834 he founded the Grand National Consolidated Trade Union.[1]

The attitude of authority towards these early trades unions is shown in the case of the six Dorset labourers who tried in 1835 to form a branch of the Agricultural Labourers' Union at Tolpuddle. Wages were 10s. a week in the next county, where the labourers were in the union, and only 7s. in Dorset. Charged under an obsolete Act with the crime of administering an oath, they were found guilty and sentenced to seven years' transportation.

A. CHARTISM

The failure of industrial organizations to improve conditions encouraged the working classes to agitate for political reform. From 1838 to 1848 interest centres in the Chartist movement (see inset map). Its failure marks the end of labour-movements which had a revolutionary character. The repeal of the Corn Laws in 1846, the improvements in factory conditions after 1833, and the growing prosperity of the country which followed the railway era led to lower prices, higher wages, and such an improved standard of life that Chartism lost its main stimulus—discontent.

B. TRADE UNIONS

After 1850 the new model trade unions for skilled craftsmen became a recognized part of industrial society. They were powerful national organizations, and the paid officials exercised a rigid control; their policy was founded on the recognition of the harmony between the interests of master and man; their method of settling disputes was by diplomacy and negotiation.

The rapid expansion of trade ceased about 1880, when foreign (*i.e.*, German and American) competition began to make itself felt. Employers, forced to cut their production costs in order to compete, were less disposed to consider demands for higher

---

[1] Over half a million members joined—an indication of working-class disappointment with the Reform Act of 1832. It was too loose an organization to achieve much, and sectional disunity caused collapse in face of the strong opposition of employers and the Government.

wages or shorter hours. The 'new unionism' of unskilled workers dates from the formation of the Dockers' Union in 1887. It relied on fighting the employer rather than on conciliation. A rapid expansion of trade unionism followed.

C. Growth of the Labour Party

The working classes, enfranchized since 1867, had been mainly 'Liberal' in politics, but from 1881 the tendency has been towards socialism. The first Trade Union Congress was held in 1868, but it was not until the end of the century that the Labour Representation Committee was formed (1900). The early Socialists had been intellectual and literary people. Socialism became a political force only when it had permeated the trade-union movement; this was largely the work of the Independent Labour Party, which was formed at Bradford in 1893. The Labour Party grew out of the Labour Representation Committee in 1906. The trade unions became affiliated to the party more because of the threats on their status and funds (*e.g.*, the Taff Vale judgment) than because of any conversion to the theory of socialism.

IMPERIAL EXPANSION

MAPS 25 to 34 deal with imperial affairs.

After the loss of the American colonies British statesmen were not interested in acquiring colonies, which were regarded as being expensive to protect and difficult to retain when fully developed. Most people in these years looked forward to the time when all the colonies would become independent and no longer a source of expense to the mother country.

A. THE EXPANSION OF THE EMPIRE AFTER 1815

Britain emerged from the Napoleonic Wars with a foothold in all the continents, but the settlements were merely coastal strips (see Map 6). During the nineteenth century the vast interior stretches were gradually peopled, and the rule of Britain was greatly extended.

(1) This was partly due to the great increase in the population of Britain. The industrial changes and the wars caused much unemployment, and the lot of the workers was unhappy (see Map 7).

Men were glad to emigrate to new countries where it was easy to make a livelihood, and the Government assisted them.

(2) But the desire to increase trade was the chief motive which led a nation of shopkeepers to acquire new lands.

After the abolition of the slave-trade the staple commodities carried in the eighteenth century (see Map 6) were no longer the chief cargoes. Iron, wheat, wool, minerals, and other raw materials became more important. Britain grew prosperous by exporting her coal, manufactured goods, and machinery.

(3) A further cause which led to the expansion of British colonies was a desire to suppress lawlessness and protect the natives. It was necessary, for example, to suppress slavery in the interior of Africa long after the abolition of the trade in slaves to America.

In the early years of the century a strong sense of responsibility towards the backward races was awakened. Missionaries, in their zeal to convert the heathen, opened up new territory.

B. THE EXPANSION OF THE EMPIRE AFTER 1870

Changes of profound importance took place in the second half of the nineteenth century. The *laissez-faire* attitude towards the colonies, which had existed from the break-up of the old colonial system, began to disappear and to be replaced by a policy of constructive imperialism.

(1) *Growth of nationality*. Consciousness of unity arose in the minds of the people of Canada, Australia, and New Zealand, and during this period they became ' nations.' The separate colonies combined to form each its own federal Government, with the sympathetic support of the British Parliament, which granted them Dominion status.

(2) *Effects of improved communications*. The introduction of steamships, the

85

opening of the Suez Canal, and the invention of the telegraph greatly reduced the barriers of time and space. Contact between the colonies and the mother country became much easier.

(*a*) The construction of railways had opened up the vast continental interiors and had made them for the first time economically valuable.

(*b*) Steamships had given a fresh importance to distant places.

Trade and emigration were stimulated.

Chamberlain, the historians Froude and Seeley, Rudyard Kipling, and others realized that co-operation between the members of the imperial family was now possible, and they strove to arouse among the people an affection and pride in the Empire.

(3) *Imperial rivalry and world politics.* The triumph of nationality in Germany and Italy and the humiliation of France led the statesmen of these countries to regard colonies as symbols of national greatness.

Industrial expansion proceeded rapidly in Europe and the U.S.A., and Britain was losing the advantage of her long start in the Industrial Revolution.

European countries, late in their pursuit of empire, found that Britain had occupied most of the temperate regions of the world; the U.S.A. forbade by the Monroe doctrine any attempt to regard South America as an area for colonization. In the last quarter of the century the Great Powers entered on a feverish search for territory, particularly in Africa and Asia. Great Britain secured an important share in the division of the undeveloped areas.

C. Effects of the Opening of the Suez Canal (1869)

(1) It shortened the distances to India, Australia, and the Far East; the amount of trade with these countries increased enormously.

(2) It altered the importance of the countries and increased the strategic value of British islands in the Mediterranean.

(3) It led to the acquisition of new colonies to guard the route *via* Suez to India (*e.g.*, Cyprus, Sudan, Somaliland).

(4) It accelerated the disappearance of the sailing-ship, as only steamers could pass through the canal.

(5) It cheapened the cost of freight.

D. Benefits of British Occupation in Tropical Possessions

The most notable services British rule has conferred on tropical countries (including India) are :

(1) *Peace.* Throughout the nineteenth century British justice and the enforcement of order have kept these lawless countries free from chaos and internal strife.

(2) *Economic development.* Railways and roads have been built to improve communications; harbours have cheapened the cost of export and import; irrigation works have led to a diminution of famine.

(3) *Medical science* has checked malaria, plague, and cholera.

(4) *Agriculture and industrial development.* The countries' natural resources have been enormously developed; new crops have been introduced; insect pests have been combated; waste lands have been brought into cultivation.

NORTH AMERICA: EXPLORATION AND SETTLEMENT

THE map shows:

(*a*) The stages in the expansion of the original thirteen American colonies across the North American continent.

(*b*) The geographic factors which affected the opening up of the northern half of the continent.

A. THE EXTREME NORTH

This was partially explored in the sixteenth and seventeenth centuries in the pursuit of a north-west passage to the East. Owing to its harsh climate, its lack of minerals, and the difficulty of its communications, it has remained comparatively isolated and unsettled.

B. THE HUDSON'S BAY COMPANY

Founded in 1670, this company had a monopoly of trade round the bay, along the coasts of which they set up forts, *i.e.*, trading-stations. Their agents, in search of skins, worked their way east and west over most of the forested country.

C. THE PACIFIC AND ARCTIC COASTS

These were opened up by a rival trading-company, on behalf of which Mackenzie, Frazer, and Thompson made the exploratory journeys shown on the map.

D. THE RED RIVER COLONY

This was the first effort to settle on the open prairie (1811). The colony was founded by the Earl of Selkirk for the benefit of dispossessed Highlanders (see Map 1).

E. THE MARITIME COLONIES

(1) Newfoundland—of importance only for its fishing-grounds.

(2) Nova Scotia and the adjacent islands of Cape Breton and Prince Edward (originally French).

F. CANADA

(1) *Lower Canada* (Quebec), surrendered by France after the Seven Years' War and still French-speaking, was the most thickly populated area in British North America. The loyalty of the inhabitants was secured by the Quebec Act of 1774, which gave religious liberty to the Roman Catholics.

(2) *Upper Canada* was settled by United Empire Loyalists, *i.e.*, those Americans

MAP 25

NORTH AMERICA EXPLORATION AND SETTLEMENT

ALASKA
Russian America
bought by U.S.A
in 1867

Longitude fixed in 1825

F R O Z E N   A R C T I C   W A S T E S

Baffin Island

Davis Strait

These names commemorate 16th and 17th Century explorers who were searching for a NW Passage to Asia

Frobisher Bay

Klondike Gold field

Klondike
Gold
Rush
1877

Alexander Mackenzie 1789 hoped to find an outlet to Pacific

Cold
Barren
Empty

SHIPS OF HUDSON'S BAY COMPANY

FURS TO ENGLAND

LABRADOR

To Newfoundland 1809

1793 crossed Rocky Peace to Pacific

Mackenzie

Trading Posts on Bay Coast

Blankets,
Guns and Powder
Knives · Sugar · Tea
Spirits

York Factory

Fort Severn

Fort Albany

Fort Charles

NEWFOUNDLAND 1713

VANCOUVER ISLAND

CANADIAN PACIFIC RAILWAY COMPLETED 1886

1811 WINNIPEG [Fort Garry]

Important fisheries the principal resource of earliest settlers

Capt. Vancouver 1791

Columbia R

Thompson 1811

Thompson 1817

49°N fixed as frontier 1818 as far as Rocky Mtns

LOWER CANADA French speaking

LOYAL COLONISTS AFTER 1783

MAINE Boundary dispute settled by Ashburton Treaty 1842.

SOUTHERN PART of OREGON TERRITORY claimed and occupied jointly by Great Britain and U.S.A
Dispute settled 1846

UPPER CANADA

P U R C H A S E D

"UNION PACIFIC" — FIRST TRANSCONTINENTAL RAILWAY COMPLETED 1869

Fort Duquesne

C E D E D

SAN FRANCISCO

California Gold rush 1846

F R O M

B Y

ORIGINAL THIRTEEN COLONIES

TERRITORY ORIGINALLY SPANISH ACQUIRED BY U.S.A FROM REPUBLICS OF TEXAS AND MEXICO 1848 and 1853

N A P O L E O N
1 8 0 3

to secure port of NEW ORLEANS at mouth of Mississippi

GT BRITAIN
1783
AFTER WAR OF INDEPENDENCE

M E X I C O

FLORIDA

purchased from Spain 1819

KEY:

CANADA:
The shading shows the Natural Vegetation only in Canada.
— Arctic wastes and tundra
≡ Forests, largely coniferous
∷ Grasslands — the prairies.
The vertical shading |·|·|·|· shows the area exploited by the HUDSON'S BAY COMPANY at the beginning of the nineteenth century.

RELIEF

PRAIRIES

who, having supported the mother country during the War of Independence, sought new homes within the Empire. They settled along the northern shores of Lake Ontario, and this area became known as 'Upper Canada.' Other loyalists went to 'Lower Canada' and to the maritime colonies.

After 1815 a constant stream of immigration from Britain made this the most populated region.

(3) *British Columbia*, until 1846, was part of Oregon, a region in the sparsely peopled mountainous West. Its ownership was long a matter of dispute between Britain and the U.S.A. The discovery of gold in 1856 brought many settlers.

(4) *The Middle States*—Manitoba, Saskatchewan, and Alberta—were part of the Hudson's Bay Company's territories until 1869. Until the construction of the Canadian Pacific Railway they did not attract many settlers.

MAP 26

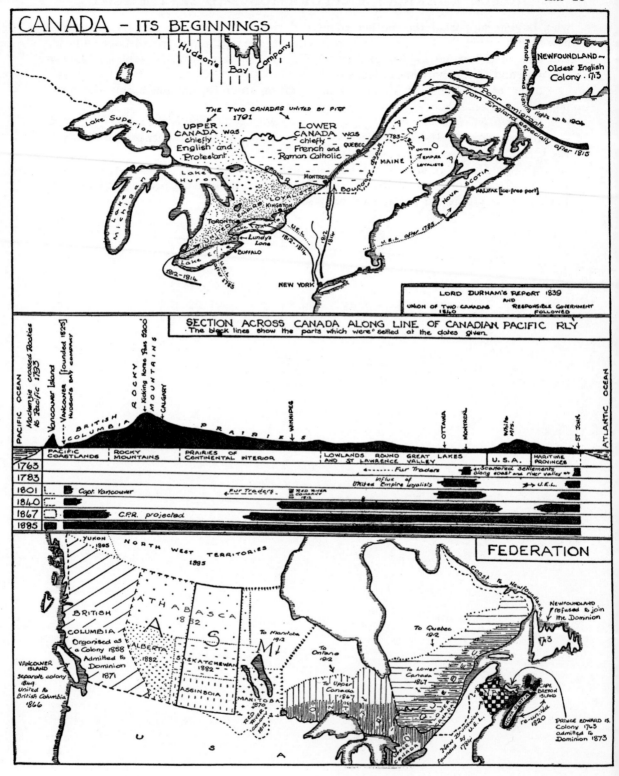

THE GROWTH OF THE DOMINION OF CANADA

A. Beginnings

THE nucleus of the Dominion was the area consisting of the old French Province of Quebec and the settlement of the United Empire Loyalists in Upper Canada.

The loyalists and the French failed to agree, and in 1791 Pitt's Canada Act created two separate provinces, each with its own elected assembly. The success of this Act was proved during the American War (1812–1814), when the French repulsed the American invasion.

B. Rebellions of 1837

(1) Discontent arose in both provinces because their assemblies were overruled by the Governors and their officials, who were always Englishmen appointed by the Colonial Office in London.

(2) The difference in race between the elected Parliament of Lower Canada and the Governor's officials increased this friction.

(3) A group of privileged families in Upper Canada (termed the ' Family Compact ') monopolized power.

(4) A further cause of discontent was the privileged position of the Anglican Church. Land was set apart in each province for the clergy.

This discontent led, after many quarrels, to a rebellion in each province. The rebellions were easily suppressed, but the Whig Government determined to investigate their causes. Lord Durham was appointed commissioner.

The Durham Report. With the help of his secretaries, Gibbon Wakefield and Charles Buller, Lord Durham drew up his famous report of 1839. He recommended :

(a) The union of the two provinces, so that the two races could learn to co-operate.

(b) Responsible government. This meant that the ministers should be responsible to the elected assemblies as the English Cabinet is responsible to the Parliament at Westminster.

The report looked forward to the time when all the provinces of British North America should be united, and, as a stimulus to this, it suggested the construction of a railway across the continent.

C. The Canada Reunion Act of 1840 and Responsible Government

This Act carried into effect the first provision of the Durham Report and united the two provinces under one Governor-general and one assembly, composed of an equal number of representatives from each province.

The other recommendation was applied by Lord Elgin, son-in-law of Lord Durham, who, as Governor-general, adopted the practice of choosing ministers from the party which had a majority in the Assembly. The maritime provinces also obtained responsible self-government in the 'forties.

D. THE FEDERATION OF CANADA

A number of factors led to federation.

(1) The 1840 Act had worked successfully until a rush of immigrants in the 'fifties made the English more numerous than the French, and racial jealousy began again. A solution of the difficulty was seen to be in the separation of the two provinces for local purposes.

(2) There was some danger of the U.S.A. acquiring control of the western province.

(3) About the same time the maritime states began to discuss among themselves a form of union.

Sir John Macdonald realized that all these conditions afforded an opportunity of forming a union of the provinces of British North America. His proposals resulted in the passing of the British North America Act of 1867. The terms of the Act :

(1) The creation of the Dominion of Canada, consisting of four provinces : Quebec, Ontario, New Brunswick, and Nova Scotia.

(2) Each province retained its separate Parliament to deal with local affairs.

(3) One Union Parliament was created for the whole Dominion, with more power than the local parliaments.

(4) Provision was made in the Act for the expansion of the union. British Columbia joined in 1871 on condition that a trans-continental railway was constructed (the C.P.R., completed in 1885). The prairie provinces in the region from Ontario to the Rockies were formed after the railway had opened up this continental area.

E. NOTE ON FRONTIER-PROBLEMS

There are no natural boundaries to divide Canada from its republican neighbour, and arbitrary political frontiers had to be negotiated, sometimes not without difficulties.

(1) *Lord Castlereagh* made an agreement in 1818 fixing the line of latitude 49° from the Lake of the Woods to the Rockies ; both parties agreed to withdraw warships from the Great Lakes.

(2) *Maine.* The frontier east of the Great Lakes had not been defined satisfactorily, and disputes arose when the region developed. In 1842 Peel's ministry yielded its claims to the U.S.A. by the Ashburton Treaty.

(3) *Oregon.* The frontier west of the Rockies was not defined until 1846. A dispute between Peel's ministry and President Polk was finally settled by an agreement to extend the frontier along the forty-ninth parallel to the Pacific.

The peaceful settlement of a 4000-mile undefended frontier is an outstanding achievement of modern history.

AUSTRALIA

A. Late Discovery of Australia

THIS great continent of the southern hemisphere was unknown to Europeans until the seventeenth century, though maps of the Middle Ages had indicated a great land-mass in the southern seas.

(1) Portuguese and Spaniards first explored the Pacific, but they were chiefly interested in the new routes to India and China and were not concerned with the 'unknown land' of the south.

(2) The most famous of the early navigators was a Dutchman, Tasman, who sailed right round Australia and discovered Van Dieman's Land (which was later called Tasmania) and New Zealand. The Dutch did not pursue their exploration, as the islands were obviously not the rich trading-lands they sought.

(3) Activity by the French led to the expeditions of Captain Cook, who in three voyages (1768–1779) explored the coasts systematically. He took possession of New South Wales in the name of Britain.

B. Development

(1) The British Government, forced by the loss of the American colonies to find a new home for convicts, decided to send them to New South Wales. (Captain Phillip arrived at Sydney with the first batch in 1788.) The laziness and insubordination of the convicts hampered the progress of the colony. Free settlers were encouraged to emigrate, but not many were attracted until the development of sheep-farming. By 1830 free settlers were in a majority.

(2) There were many difficulties in the way of exploration of the interior.

(a) The Eastern Highlands proved difficult to cross, and settlement was restricted to the coastal regions.

(b) The climate of the interior was unfavourable. Long droughts were followed by sudden storms and dangerous floods. The map shows that much of the interior and the west is too dry for agriculture.

(c) The grazing-lands of the Murray-Darling Basin were explored and used by 'squatters' from 1813. Spanish merino sheep, introduced on coastlands in 1803, found ideal conditions on these grassy plains where they were reared after 1830.

(3) Other convict settlements were made at :

(a) *Hobart*, in Van Dieman's Land, in 1803. The most desperate criminals were sent here.

(b) *Brisbane*, in what is now called Queensland.

(c) *Melbourne*. Settlers from Van Dieman's Land and pioneers from New South Wales settled this area, now known as Victoria.

N.B. These places, originally part of New South Wales, became the nuclei of distinct colonies. Difficulties of communication made separate administration inevitable.

(4) The first free settlement was established in Western Australia along the Swan

MAP 27

AUSTRALIA

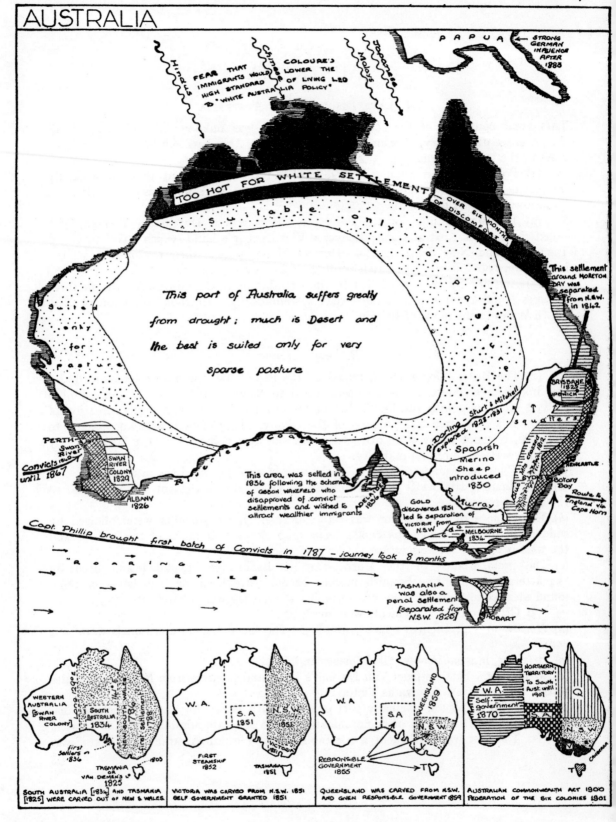

STRONG GERMAN INFLUENCE AFTER 1885

P A P U A

FEAR THAT CHINESE COLOURED IMMIGRANTS WOULD LOWER THE HIGH STANDARD OF LIVING LED TO "WHITE AUSTRALIA POLICY"

Hindus   Chinese   Malays   Japanese

TOO HOT FOR WHITE SETTLEMENT — OVER SIX MONTHS OF DISCOMFORT

Suitable only for p...

This settlement around MORETON BAY was separated from N.S.W. in 1842

Suited only for pasture

This part of Australia suffers greatly from drought; much is Desert and the best is suited only for very sparse pasture

BRISBANE 1825 Ipswich

squatters

R. Darling — Sturt & Mitchell explored 1828-1831

Spanish Merino Sheep introduced 1830

PERTH Swan River
Convicts until 1867

SWAN RIVER COLONY 1829

ALBANY 1826

This area was settled in 1836 following the scheme of GIBBON WAKEFIELD who disapproved of convict settlements and wished to attract wealthier immigrants

ADELAIDE 1836

R. Murray

GOLD discovered 1851 led to separation of VICTORIA from N.S.W.

MELBOURNE 1834

NEWCASTLE

SYDNEY Botany Bay
Route to England via Cape Horn

Capt. Phillip brought first batch of Convicts in 1787 — journey took 8 months

"R O A R I N G   F O R T I E S"

TASMANIA was also a penal settlement [separated from N.S.W. 1825]

HOBART

WESTERN AUSTRALIA [SWAN RIVER COLONY]

SOUTH AUSTRALIA 1834

NEW SOUTH WALES first settlement 1788

first settlers in 1836

TASMANIA OR VAN DIEMAN'S L.D 1825

1803

SOUTH AUSTRALIA [1834] AND TASMANIA [1825] WERE CARVED OUT OF NEW S WALES.

W. A.

S.A. 1851

N.S.W. 1851

VICTORIA 1851

TASMANIA 1851

FIRST STEAMSHIP 1852

VICTORIA WAS CARVED FROM N.S.W. 1851 SELF GOVERNMENT GRANTED 1851

W. A

S A

QUEENSLAND 1859

N.S.W.

RESPONSIBLE GOVERNMENT 1855

T

QUEENSLAND WAS CARVED FROM N.S.W. AND GIVEN RESPONSIBLE GOVERNMENT 1859

W. A. Self-government 1870

NORTHERN TERRITORY To South Aust. until 1907

Q

S A

N.S.W.

V

Canberra

T

AUSTRALIAN COMMONWEALTH ACT 1900 FEDERATION OF THE SIX COLONIES 1901

River (1829). The colony did not prosper until after 1849, when the landowners had petitioned for convicts.

(5) An experiment in colonization on the lines suggested by Gibbon Wakefield was organized in 1836 in South Australia. Wakefield opposed convict-settlements and suggested that :

(a) Free grants of land were disastrous to successful colonization.

(b) Land should be sold at a uniform price and sufficiently high to discourage the purchase of holdings which were too large to be worked properly.

(c) Emigration should be assisted from the proceeds of the sale of land.

Adelaide was the site chosen for the capital of the colony. The results of the experiment were disappointing. The high price of land discouraged settlers. The firmness and enterprise of the Governor, Sir George Grey (1841–1845), saved the colony from ruin.

(6) The interior of Australia remained undeveloped owing to the desert conditions ; the northern part of the continent also proved unsuitable ; its hot, wet climate made white settlement too difficult.

C. The Commonwealth of Australia

(1) By 1859 practically the whole of the continent had been explored.

(2) The convict-system had come to an end owing to the objections of the free settlers.

(3) Gold was discovered, and the population rapidly increased. Agriculture—especially sheep-farming—became more profitable.

(4) After the abolition of the convict-system all the colonies, except Western Australia, were granted representative government (1851) followed by responsible government (1855).

(5) Each colony developed along its own lines, and jealousies divided the Australian people. New South Wales, the mother colony, claimed precedence. All the colonies were unwilling to surrender their independence until towards the end of the century.

(a) Fear of the advance of foreign powers in the Pacific showed the need for a common policy of defence—e.g., German annexation of part of New Guinea and the Pacific Islands, and the rise of Japan.

(b) The vacant north of Australia was climatically suited to the people of over-crowded India, China, and Japan. Fearing the competition of cheap coloured labour, the Australians united in a common policy of resistance to coloured immigrants.

(c) Internal difficulties arose (e.g., tariff barriers and railway systems on different gauges), and exposed the folly of separatism.

(d) The individual colonies had difficulty in raising the capital necessary to finance the full development of the continent.

(6) The Commonwealth of Australia Act (1900) created a central Government, which elected a Senate and House of Representatives to deal with defence, commerce, postal systems, railways, immigration, and currency. Each state retained its own Parliament and Government to deal with all other questions.

MAP 28

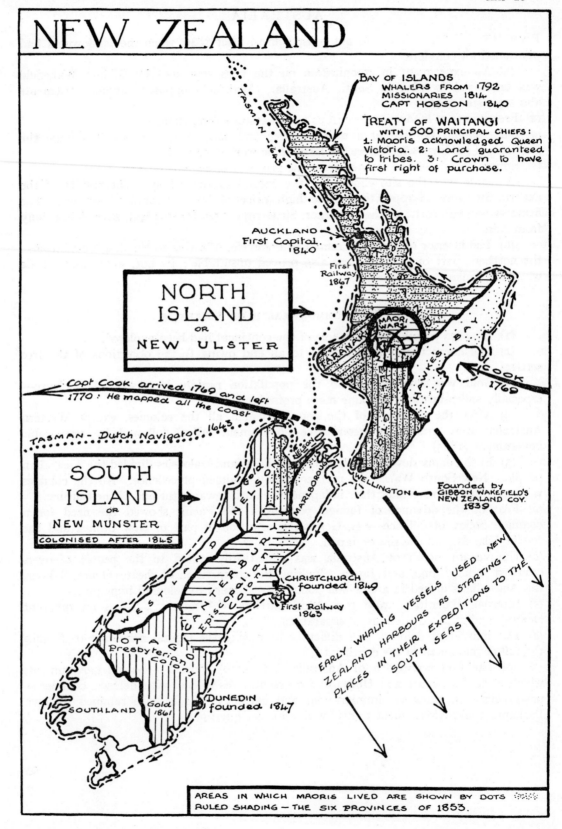

NEW ZEALAND

BAY of ISLANDS
WHALERS FROM 1792
MISSIONARIES 1814
CAPT HOBSON 1840

TREATY of WAITANGI
WITH 500 PRINCIPAL CHIEFS:
1: Maoris acknowledged Queen
Victoria. 2: Land guaranteed
to tribes. 3: Crown to have
first right of purchase.

TASMAN SEA 1643

AUCKLAND
First Capital.
1840

First
Railway
1867

MAORI
WARS

NORTH
ISLAND
OR
NEW ULSTER

TARANAKI

WELLINGTON

HAWKES BAY

COOK
1769

Capt Cook arrived 1769 and left
1770 : He mapped all the coast

TASMAN — Dutch Navigator. 1643

NELSON

MARLBOROUGH

SOUTH
ISLAND
OR
NEW MUNSTER
COLONISED AFTER 1845

NELSON

WESTLAND

CANTERBURY
Episcopalian Colony

WELLINGTON

Founded by
GIBBON WAKEFIELD'S
NEW ZEALAND COY.
1839

CHRISTCHURCH
founded 1849

First Railway
1863

OTAGO
Presbyterian
Colony

EARLY WHALING VESSELS USED NEW
ZEALAND HARBOURS AS STARTING-
PLACES IN THEIR EXPEDITIONS TO THE
SOUTH SEAS

SOUTHLAND

Gold
1861

DUNEDIN
founded 1847

AREAS IN WHICH MAORIS LIVED ARE SHOWN BY DOTS
RULED SHADING — THE SIX PROVINCES OF 1853.

NEW ZEALAND

A. EARLY HISTORY

AT the beginning of the seventeenth century the Dutch navigator, Tasman, sailing the southern seas, discovered the South Island of New Zealand. But as it could not satisfy their desires for spices and tropical produce, the Dutch took little interest in the discovery.

In 1769 Captain Cook claimed New Zealand for Britain. The islands were fertile and attracted a mixed group of settlers, traders, whalers (who met at the Bay of Islands as early as 1792), runaway convicts, and seamen. These made a home among the Maoris, the intelligent but warlike savages who lived in the islands. Missionaries came, too, and in 1814 they founded a station at the Bay of Islands ; they had great influence on the natives and did much to civilize them.

B. ANNEXATION BY THE BRITISH GOVERNMENT

During the period of this early settlement the Government took no steps to establish any effective control. In 1840 the home Government at length resolved to intervene because :

(1) Friction between the white settlers and the natives led to bloodshed and disorder. Lands were taken from the natives unfairly, and firearms were given in exchange.

(2) French companies had been formed to colonize the South Island, and there was a danger of French annexation.

(3) Gibbon Wakefield maintained that New Zealand was " the fittest country in the world for colonization." He urged the Government to act. The New Zealand Association was founded to buy lands on which to settle emigrants.

In 1840 the Governor of New South Wales was instructed to take over the colony. By the Treaty of Waitangi Captain Hobson received the submission of the chiefs, who were allowed to retain their lands. Shortly afterwards New Zealand was declared a separate colony, and Auckland became its capital.

C. DIFFICULTIES WITH THE NATIVES

(1) Wakefield's New Zealand Company, which had settled Wellington, Taranaki, and Nelson, ignored the Treaty of Waitangi and continued to bargain with the natives for land.

(2) The natives were difficult to subdue ; they loved fighting and were quarrelsome and disorderly.

D. SIR GEORGE GREY : GOVERNOR-GENERAL (1848–1853)

Sir George Grey settled these difficulties and thereby laid the foundation of the colony's prosperity.

(1) He upheld the rights of the natives and stopped the sale of firearms.

G

(2) He solved the land-question by purchasing from the native chiefs the land unoccupied by them. (*N.B.* This was mainly in South Island. It was occupied by Anglican and Scottish Presbyterian settlers. The New Zealand Company was dissolved in 1853.)

(3) He won the loyalty of the natives, who recognized the justice of his rule.

(4) He advised the granting of representative assemblies.

E. MAORI WARS (1860–1871)

Sir George Grey had settled the native problem in the South Island, which was rapidly populated by English settlers.

In the North Island, however, the greater part of the interior of the country still belonged to the tribes. Disputes about land which the colonial Parliament confiscated caused conflict. The Maoris united to acknowledge the rule of an elected king. Revolts lasted for ten years and hampered the development of the island. At the end of the wars the Maoris held more than half of the island, and they still do so to-day.

F. GOVERNMENT OF THE COLONY

1853. The six provinces held elected assemblies ; there was a General Assembly for the whole colony.

1856. Responsible government was granted.

1876. Provincial assemblies were abolished.

1901. New Zealand refused to join the newly formed Commonwealth of Australia.

1907. New Zealand was given the status of ' Dominion.'

THE GROWTH OF BRITISH POWER IN INDIA

THE map shows the main stages in the growth of British power in India. The area shaded black represents the possessions of the East India Company in 1783. Various line shadings show the growth of territory during the century. The areas left blank are the ' native states ' which are nominally independent ; they manage their own local affairs, but a British Resident gives advice, and they acknowledge the supremacy of the British Raj in external affairs.

A. THE EAST INDIA COMPANY

(1) *Trade.* In 1783 the East India, or ' John,' Company was still primarily a trading-company, with directors interested mainly in dividends. Its monopoly was not withdrawn until 1813 ; a great expansion of trade followed.

(a) Lancashire merchants began the export of manufactured cotton goods to the undeveloped Indian market.

(b) Planters, hitherto forbidden by the company, went out to settle and began the cultivation of cotton, tea, and sugar.

(c) Trade was also stimulated by the removal of internal tariff barriers as the native states were absorbed during the nineteenth century.

(2) *Problems of administering territory.* The East India Company administered large territories in India. Two great perils had confronted the company in the early eighteenth century :

(a) Lawlessness and violence that followed the decay of the Mogul Empire.

(b) French ambition to expel the British traders from India.

In self-preservation the British had been forced to overthrow the French and to take responsibility for the government of certain areas, viz. :

(a) Bengal—a province as large as the British Isles.

(b) The Madras district of the Carnatic.

(c) The coastal strip known as the Circars, which linked Bengal with the Carnatic.

(d) The island of Bombay, with a small coastal area on the mainland opposite.

With the acquisition of Bengal in 1763 it was clearly the duty of the Crown to relieve the company of its burden of ruling these areas. Lord North's Regulating Act (1773) had given the Crown the right to nominate a Governor-general. The difficult position of Warren Hastings, the first nominee, showed that the Act was inadequate. Pitt's India Act in 1784 set up a Board of Control in London and increased the powers of the Governor-general. Thus was created the dual system which lasted until the mutiny ; the company conducted the commercial affairs, and the board controlled the administration in the name of the directors.

B. THE NATIVE STATES

The Mohammedan Emperor, the Mogul, lived in Delhi and still nominally controlled all India ; but his Empire had broken up into a large number of independent

MAP 29

GROWTH of BRITISH POWER in INDIA

AFGHANISTAN

BALUCHISTAN

KASHMIR

TIBET

Annexed after the
SIKH WARS 1845-49

PUNJAB

Ceded by NEPAL to the
Marquis Hastings
1815

NEPAL

UPPER
BURMA
annexed 1886

Ceded after the
FIRST BURMESE WAR 1824
Lord Amherst: Governor-
General

ASSAM

Ceded by the Nawab of OUDH
to the Marquis Wellesley
1802

OUDH
annexed
1856

Ceded after
FIRST BURMESE
WAR, 1824
Lord Amherst
Gov. General
1803

NORTH WEST PROVINCES [AGRA PROVINCE]

BENGAL

Ceded by BONSLA
to the Marquis
Wellesley
1803

BIHAR

PEGU

Ceded after
SECOND BURMESE
WAR, 1852
Marquis of Dalhousie
Governor-General

Ceded after the
FIRST BURMESE WAR, 1824

RAJPUTANA

SIND

Annexed by
Hardinge
1843

SCINDIA

CENTRAL PROVINCES

BERAR

1803

NIZAMS DOMINIONS

1803

Annexed by the
Marquis of Hastings
after the MAHRATTA
WAR 1816-1818

BOMBAY

GOA
[Portuguese]

MYSORE

Ser

Acquired after the
Second Mysore War
1780-1792
Governor-General:
Marquis Cornwallis

MADRAS

Acquired after the
Conquest of Mysore 1799
by the Marquis Wellesley

TRAVANCORE

CEYLON

occupied 1796
ceded to Britain by
Treaty of Amiens
1802

LIMIT of MAHRATTA DOMINATION
SHOWN BY THICK BLACK LINE

KEY

CLIVE &
WARREN HASTINGS

CORNWALLIS

WELLESLEY

HASTINGS

AMHERST

HARDINGE

DALHOUSIE

kingdoms, whose rivalry and conflict made possible and inevitable the extension of British influence.

The chief groups of native states were :

(1) The *Carnatic*, whose Nawab relied upon the support of the British at Madras.

(2) *Mysore*.   Ruled by an ambitious Mohammedan prince, Tipoo Sultan.

(3) *Hyderabad*.   Ruled by a Mohammedan prince known as the Nizam.

(4) A group of allied Hindu *Mahratta States* in Central India.   A black line on the map limits the area they controlled.

(5) *Punjab*.   In North-west India, in possession of the Sikhs, a sect of Hindus, who were beginning to form a united nation.

(6) *Sind*.   In the lower Indus valley, ruled by a group of princes owning allegiance to the Afghans.

(7) *Rohilkhand*.   In the Upper Ganges Valley, in which a band of Afghan raiders had established themselves in the eighteenth century.

(8) *Oudh*.   Another province in the Ganges Valley, whose rulers had made themselves independent of the Mogul Emperors early in the eighteenth century.

In addition to the above there were three frontier states outside India proper :

(9) *Afghanistan*.   Afghan attacks had brought about the final ruin of the Mogul Empire.   At one time they had made themselves masters of the whole of North-west India, but at the beginning of the nineteenth century they had withdrawn to their native hills.   They still controlled all the mountain passes of North-west India.

(10) *Nepal*.   In the Himalayas, the territory of the warlike Gurkhas.

(11) *Burma*.   The Burmese were a different race from the Indians.   They came into conflict with the British when they invaded Assam.

C. British Conquests in the Nineteenth Century

Despite a keen reluctance to engage in war or to acquire territory, the East India Company, faced with the anarchy which resulted from the decay of the Mogul Empire, was compelled to put down disorder in neighbouring states, for threats to peace were hindrances to trade.

(1) *Marquis of Wellesley* (1798–1805)

(a) He extended British power by concluding alliances with the weaker native rulers, whereby the company made itself responsible for the defence of the state.

(b) He attacked and defeated Tipoo of Mysore, annexing lands on both east and west coasts and restoring what remained to a former Hindu ruler, with whom he concluded an alliance.

(c) The Nazim of Hyderabad was forced to disband his troops and subordinate himself to the British.

(d) The Madras Presidency was enlarged by the addition of the Carnatic, and Bombay by the Surat and surrounding lands ; the rulers received compensation.

(e) The Nawab of Oudh, the oldest ally of Britain, whose kingdom was badly misgoverned and was too weak to withstand attack, was forced to surrender part of his territory.

(f) Only the Mahrattas remained strong enough to dispute the supremacy of Britain. They were too independent to accept treaties of alliance.   Wellesley began the process of subjection by force, helped by his brother, the future Duke of Wellington, who won a victory at Assaye in 1802.

(2) *Marquis of Hastings* (1813–1823)

(*a*) He extended the work of Wellesley, completing the destruction of the Mahratta Confederacy ; he annexed Poona and forced the Hindu chiefs to admit defeat.

(*b*) He defeated the Gurkhas of Nepal.

(*c*) He annihilated the Pindaris, robber bands which disturbed the peace of Central India.

(3) *Extension of India's frontiers*

By 1823 all India was directly or indirectly under British control ; thereafter expansion was at the expense of the frontier states.

(*a*) Between the years 1823–1857 Britain annexed the coast and southern part of Burma, and the rest of the country in 1886, when King Thibaw intrigued with the French.

(*b*) The most serious problems concerned the north-west, beyond which lay *Afghanistan*. All British statesmen were alive to the danger of a foreign power securing influence in Afghanistan.

There were two main routes from India :

    (i) South through Sind and the Bolan Pass.

    (ii) North through the Punjab and the Khyber Pass.

In 1843 the British annexed Sind in order to control the southern route.

The Sikhs, who ruled the Punjab, were alarmed and, underrating the British military power after the Afghan disaster of 1841, crossed the frontier from the Punjab. Two Sikh wars were fought, after which the Punjab was annexed by Dalhousie in 1849.

THE INDIAN MUTINY

A. Causes

(1) *Reforms.* From the time when Lord Bentinck (1828–1835) strove to improve conditions in India until Lord Dalhousie (1848–1856) introduced western reforms on a large scale, there had been growing in the minds of a people unaccustomed to change a profound uneasiness. Changes which developed the resources of the country and the efficacy of the Government were not appreciated by the natives, whose traditions and customs were ruthlessly set aside.

N.B. Bentinck's reforms :

(a) The abolition of *suttee*, the practice of burning widows.

(b) The suppression of the *thugs*, a sect of assassins.

(c) The introduction of an English educational system. This was encouraged by Lord Macaulay. English has become the international language of India, a land of a hundred different tongues.

(d) The opening up of the lower ranks of the Indian Civil Service to natives.

(e) The drawing up of the Indian code of law.

Previously the company, anxious only for trade, had respected the religious and social customs of the Indians. Bentinck's changes mark the beginning of a humanitarian outlook.

(2) *Annexations.* Extensive annexations seriously undermined the loyalty of the Indian Princes. Dalhousie, convinced of the benefits of British rule, extended the boundaries of the company's dominions by the annexation of numerous misgoverned native states (see map). He seized those states whose rulers died without heirs, ignoring the Hindu custom, which permitted an adopted son to succeed. Seven states thus lapsed to the company.

He deposed the King of Oudh in 1856.

(3) *Discontent in the native army.* The sepoys—*i.e.*, Indian native soldiers disciplined in European methods of fighting—were mostly recruited from Bengal and Oudh. They objected to service in distant foreign lands as this involved loss of caste.[1]

(4) *Religious unrest.* There was a widespread fear that Christianity was to be forced on the natives, partly due to missionary activity and partly to the introduction of European customs.

(5) *Immediate causes*

(a) The mutiny occurred after a regulation had been issued directing the soldiers to bite the ends of cartridges used in the new Enfield rifle. The cartridges were greased with animal fat. For once the Hindus and Mohammedans were united in what they considered was an attack on their religious principles. (The cow was sacred to the Hindu and the pig unclean to the Mohammedan).

(b) The sepoys were reluctant to serve in Burma because to leave India meant loss of caste.

(c) The extensive withdrawal of British troops made the moment opportune for revolt.

[1] The proportion of Europeans to sepoys in the army was small. Troops had been withdrawn from India during the Crimean War (1854–1855) and the war in China (1857).

MAP 30

INDIAN MUTINY

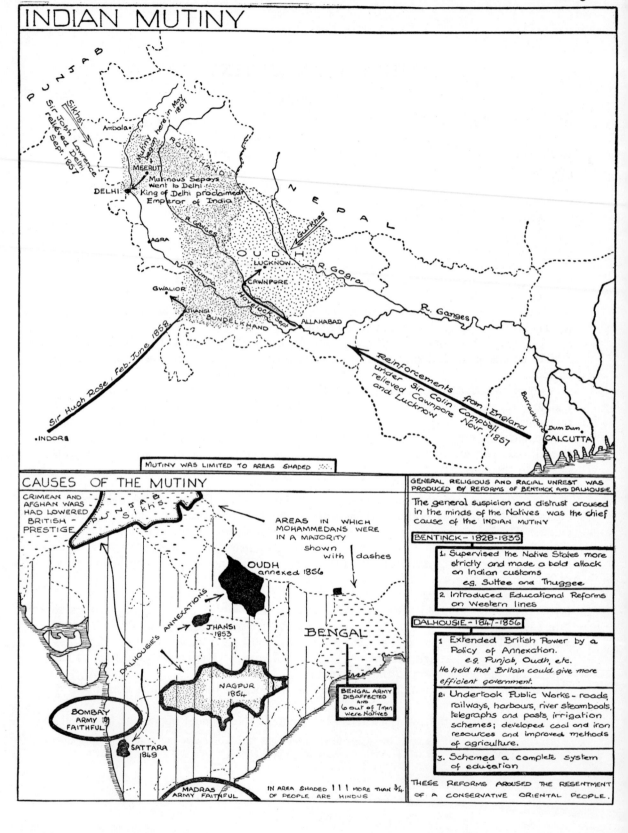

PUNJAB

Sikhs: Sir John Lawrence relieved Delhi Sept. 1857

Ambala·

Mutiny began here in May 1857

ROHILKHAND

MEERUT

DELHI

Mutinous Sepoys went to Delhi. King of Delhi proclaimed Emperor of India

R. Ganges

AGRA

R. Jumna

GWALIOR

JHANSI

BUNDELKHAND

Havelock Sept.

OUDH

LUCKNOW

CAWNPORE

ALLAHABAD

NEPAL

Gurkhas

R. Gogra

R. Ganges

Sir Hugh Rose: Feb.-June 1858

·INDORE

Reinforcements from England under Sir Colin Campbell relieved Cawnpore and Lucknow Novr. 1857

Barrackpore

Dum Dum

CALCUTTA

MUTINY WAS LIMITED TO AREAS SHADED

CAUSES OF THE MUTINY

CRIMEAN AND AFGHAN WARS HAD LOWERED BRITISH PRESTIGE

PUNJAB Sikhs

AREAS IN WHICH MOHAMMEDANS WERE IN A MAJORITY shown with dashes

OUDH annexed 1856

DALHOUSIE'S ANNEXATIONS

JHANSI 1853

BENGAL

NAGPUR 1854

BOMBAY ARMY FAITHFUL

SATTARA 1849

BENGAL ARMY DISAFFECTED AND 6 out of 7 men were Natives

MADRAS ARMY FAITHFUL

IN AREA SHADED ||| MORE THAN ¾ OF PEOPLE ARE HINDUS

GENERAL RELIGIOUS AND RACIAL UNREST WAS PRODUCED BY REFORMS OF BENTINCK AND DALHOUSIE

The general suspicion and distrust aroused in the minds of the Natives was the chief cause of the INDIAN MUTINY

BENTINCK - 1828-1835

1. Supervised the Native States more strictly and made a bold attack on Indian customs e.g. Suttee and Thuggee

2. Introduced Educational Reforms on Western lines

DALHOUSIE - 1847-1856

1. Extended British Power by a Policy of Annexation. e.g. Punjab, Oudh, etc. He held that Britain could give more efficient government.

2. Undertook Public Works - roads, railways, harbours, river steamboats, telegraphs and posts, irrigation schemes; developed coal and iron resources and improved methods of agriculture.

3. Schemed a complete system of education

THESE REFORMS AROUSED THE RESENTMENT OF A CONSERVATIVE ORIENTAL PEOPLE.

THE INDIAN MUTINY

B. The Mutiny

The map shows that the mutiny was practically confined to the Ganges Valley. The first disorders took place in the neighbourhood of Calcutta, but a more important revolt, generally regarded as the beginning of the mutiny, occurred at Meerut. The sepoys advanced to Delhi, where the restoration of the Mogul Empire was proclaimed.

The two other important centres were Cawnpore, where a Mahratta chief led a savage massacre of the European population, and Lucknow. Interest then centred in Lucknow; General Havelock captured it, but he was besieged until relieved by Sir Colin Campbell.

The turning-point of the mutiny, however, was the capture of Delhi by troops from the Punjab, collected from among the loyal Sikhs by Sir John Lawrence.

The risings continued for some months in Central India, where Sir Hugh Rose conducted the campaign in a difficult hilly country.

C. Consequences

(1) The East India Company was abolished, and its territories were transferred to the Crown. A Secretary of State for India, aided by a Council representing the Cabinet, took control of Indian affairs. In India a Viceroy represented the Queen. (In 1877 Queen Victoria took the title 'Empress of India.')

(2) Reforms were introduced more cautiously, care being taken to respect Indian customs. The doctrine of lapse was abandoned.

(3) The Indian army was reorganized, the proportion of British to native troops being increased.

Refer also to " Effects of the Opening of the Suez Canal," and " Benefits of British Occupation," p. 86.

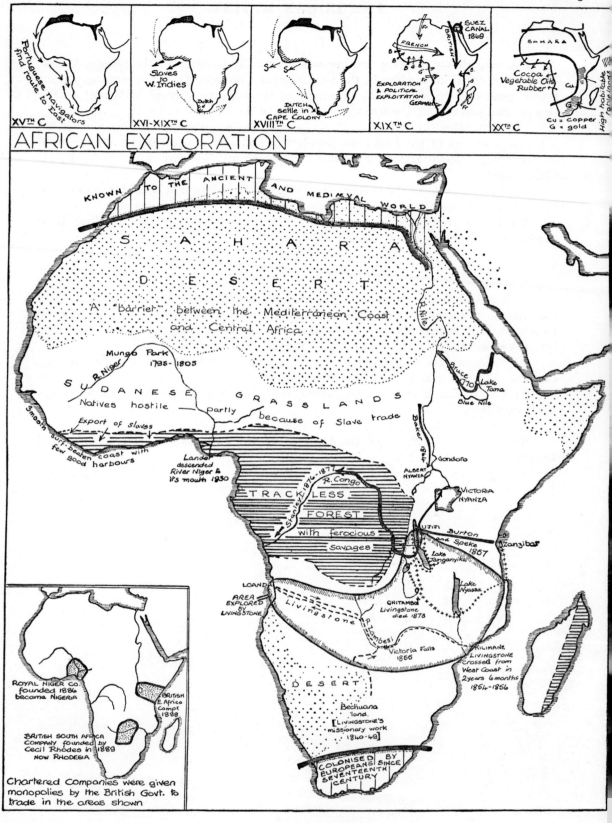

MAP 31

AFRICAN EXPLORATION

Portuguese navigators find route to East
XVᵀᴴ C

Slaves to W. Indies
Dutch
XVI-XIXᵀᴴ C

Dutch settle in Cape Colony
XVIIIᵀᴴ C

EXPLORATION & POLITICAL EXPLOITATION GERMAN
FRENCH
SUEZ CANAL 1869
XIXᵀᴴ C

SAHARA
Cocoa Vegetable Oils Rubber
Cu = Copper
G = gold
High habitable tableland
XXᵀᴴ C

KNOWN TO THE ANCIENT AND MEDIÆVAL WORLD

S A H A R A   D E S E R T

A "barrier" between the Mediterranean Coast and Central Africa

Mungo Park 1795-1805
R. Niger

S U D A N E S E   G R A S S L A N D S
Natives hostile — partly because of Slave trade

Smooth surf-beaten coast with few good harbours
Export of slaves

Lander descended River Niger to its mouth 1830

T R A C K L E S S   FOREST with ferocious Savages
Stanley 1874-1877
R. Congo

R. Nile
Bruce 1770 Lake Tana
Blue Nile

Baker 1864
Gondoro
ALBERT NYANZA
VICTORIA NYANZA

UJIJI Burton and Speke 1857 Zanzibar
Lake Tanganyika
Lake Nyassa

LOANDA
AREA EXPLORED BY LIVINGSTONE
Livingstone
CHITAMBO Livingstone died 1873

R. Zambesi
Victoria Falls 1855
KILIMANE LIVINGSTONE crossed from West Coast in 2 years 6 months 1854-1856

D E S E R T

Bechuana land
[LIVINGSTONE'S missionary work 1840-48]

COLONISED BY EUROPEANS SINCE SEVENTEENTH CENTURY

ROYAL NIGER CO. founded 1886 became NIGERIA
BRITISH E. Africa Coy. 1888
BRITISH SOUTH AFRICA COMPANY founded by Cecil Rhodes in 1889 NOW RHODESIA

Chartered Companies were given monopolies by the British Govt. to trade in the areas shown

AFRICA: EXPLORATION AND SETTLEMENT

A. AFRICA, THE 'DARK CONTINENT'

THOUGH part of the 'Old World' and the home of one of the earliest civilizations (Egypt), Africa was the last of the continents to be thoroughly explored. Its interior was so little known that it was called the 'Dark Continent.'

B. DIFFICULTIES OF EXPLORATION AND SETTLEMENT

The reasons why the interior of Africa remained for so long unknown are mainly geographical.

(1) *Shape*

(*a*) Its coast is smooth and regular; there are few bays or gulfs which would provide harbours for shipping, facilitate penetration to the interior, and ameliorate the climate by enabling maritime influences to spread inland. The many formidable obstacles along the coast are shown on the map.

(*b*) There is a shortage of islands along the coast—island bases which would have served as jumping-off grounds for the operations of early explorers. (*Cp.* use made of Zanzibar, one of the few coastal islands.)

(2) *Structure*

Africa is a high tableland. Because of the high land near the edge of the continent two things happen.

(*a*) Waterfalls and rapids occur in all the rivers near their mouths. Hence penetration by rivers—the usual method of entering continental interiors—is impossible, and railway construction to avoid the rapids is also difficult.

(*b*) On-shore winds bring excessive rain to the coastal slopes, but the inland areas are, correspondingly, too dry.

(3) *Climate*

Africa lies largely within the tropics. The areas climatically suited to white settlement are:

(*a*) The Mediterranean coast-lands.

(*b*) The southern tip (Dutch settlements after the seventeenth century).

(*c*) Parts of the high plateau, where altitude counteracts the effects of latitude (*e.g.*, parts of Kenya Colony).

The moist heat of equatorial Africa debilitates white men—*i.e.*, it makes them disinclined to do any work.

(4) *Insects and disease*

(*a*) Disease-carrying insects bite and sting in the hot and damp regions; they pollute food; they creep under the skin to lay their eggs. They transmit disease—*e.g.*, malaria and elephantiasis, carried by the mosquito, and sleeping-sickness, transmitted by the tsetse fly.

(*b*) Crops are ruined (locusts), buildings and any woodwork are eaten away (white ants), while the tsetse-fly plays havoc with beasts of burden.

(5) *Difficulties of Transport*

(a) A desert in the north and a vast forest in the centre made transport difficult.

(b) There was an absence of animals which could have been used for transport—only the camel in the north and oxen in tsetse-free areas. The native elephant was untameable.

(c) African animals proved worse than useless: monkeys pulled up field crops; elephants trampled them down; and lions and leopards consumed any domestic animals, children, women, or old men who might have escaped the insect peril.

(d) The native porters on which the white man was forced to rely for transport were unreliable and slow.

(6) *Hostility of native population*

(a) The natives were hostile; the most fertile parts of the continent were the most unhealthy, and therefore were avoided by the native tribes, who were forced to live in the areas where cultivation was most difficult and food more restricted—a possible cause of their cannibalism (*cp.* the undersized, treacherous, and degraded pygmies met by Stanley in the Congo forest).

(b) The slave-trade led to suspicion of the motives of white traders and missionaries.

(c) There was no common native language that explorers could use.

(7) *Lack of incentive to explore the interior*

(a) The savage population did not want European manufactures, and with the passing of the slave-trade (men for spirits and guns) there was no material to exchange.

(b) The demand for tropical produce in Europe and North America—*e.g.*, rubber, coco-nut oil—had not arisen.

(c) The slave-trade, which had prospered from the sixteenth century, did not require any exploration, for the slave-trading companies bought slaves from regular dealers who worked in the interior.

C. British Exploration in Africa

(1) *The Nile basin.* As early as 1770 James Bruce, a Consul of Algiers, interested himself in the source of the Nile and its annual flood. He made the journey shown on the map and discovered the source of the Blue Nile.

Richard Burton and J. H. Speke, on behalf of the Royal Geographical Society, set out to discover the source of the White Nile. They discovered Lake Tanganyika in 1854. When Speke found Victoria Nyanza, the source of the Nile was no longer a mystery. Sir S. Baker made a systematic exploration of the Upper Nile valley and found other sources of the great river in the Lake Albert, which he discovered in 1864.

(2) *The Niger basin.* Mungo Park (1795–1805), starting from Gambia, traced the course of the Upper Niger. He passed Timbuktu, but failed to solve the problem as to where the river reached the ocean. His party was greatly reduced owing to malaria, and he was slain by the hostile natives. The Lander brothers showed that the swamps at the head of the Gulf of Guinea were really the mouth of the Niger.

(3) *The Zambesi basin.* Livingstone (1813–1873) was the greatest of all African explorers. He was sent out by the London Missionary Society and started missionary work in Bechuanaland in 1840. He continued his medical mission work until 1856.

During this time he explored the upper waters of the Zambesi and crossed Africa from coast to coast.

In 1858, at the head of a Government expedition, he discovered Lake Nyassa. He denounced the atrocities of the slave-trade. On his last journey (1866–1873), starting from Lake Tanganyika, he mapped the area which included the Upper Congo and East Central Africa.

(4) *The Congo basin*. H. M. Stanley set out in 1871 in search of Livingstone, who had sent no news of his progress. Later Stanley made his name famous by his exploration of the Congo (1874–1878). In his book *Through Darkest Africa* he disclosed to the world the wealth of raw materials which the Congo basin would yield, and the scramble for Africa quickly followed.

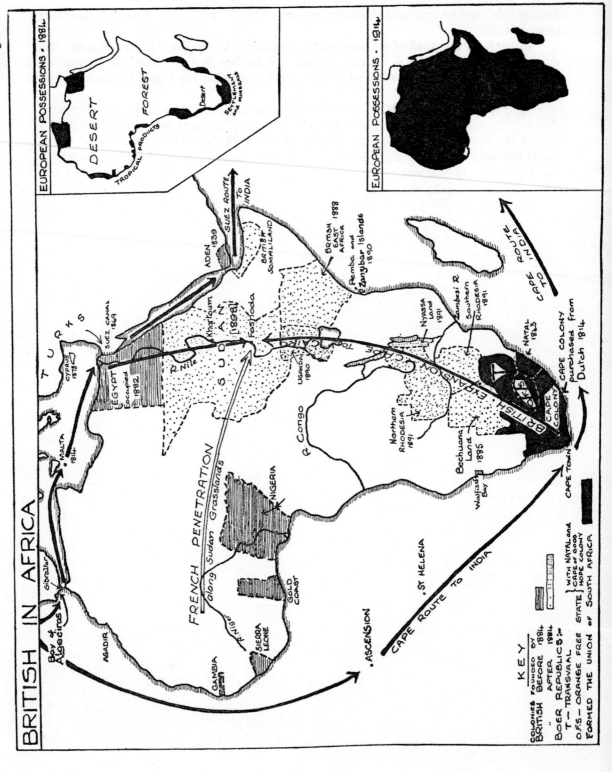

MAP 32

BRITISH IN AFRICA

EUROPEAN POSSESSIONS · 1884

DESERT

FOREST

TROPICAL PRODUCTS

Desert

SETTLEMENT and MINERALS

EUROPEAN POSSESSIONS · 1914

Bay of Algeciras
Gibraltar
AGADIR
TURKS
MALTA 1814
CYPRUS 1878
SUEZ CANAL 1869
EGYPT Occupied 1882
R. Nile
ADEN 1839
SUEZ ROUTE To INDIA
BRITISH SOMALILAND
Khartoum
SUDAN 1898
Fashoda
BRITISH EAST AFRICA 1888
Pemba and Zanzibar Islands 1890
GAMBIA
SIERRA LEONE
R. Niger
FRENCH PENETRATION Along Sudan Grasslands
NIGERIA
GOLD COAST
R. Congo
UGANDA 1840
CAIRO
BRITISH EXPANSION
Northern Rhodesia 1891
Bechuana Land 1885
Walfisch Bay
NYASSA LAND 1891
Zambesi R.
Southern RHODESIA 1891
T
O.F.S
CAPE COLONY
NATAL 1843
CAPE COLONY purchased from Dutch 1814
CAPE TOWN
. ST HELENA
. ASCENSION
CAPE ROUTE TO INDIA
CAPE ROUTE TO INDIA

KEY
COLONIES FOUNDED BY BRITISH BEFORE 1884
" " AFTER 1884
BOER REPUBLICS:—
T.— TRANSVAAL
O.F.S.— ORANGE FREE STATE
WITH NATAL and CAPE of GOOD HOPE COLONY FORMED THE UNION OF SOUTH AFRICA

THE BRITISH IN AFRICA

The map shows the great extent of territory that Britain acquired in Africa. The inset maps indicate the importance of the period after 1880.

Though Britain was the last of the Western European nations to join the ' scramble ' for unoccupied territory in the 'eighties, her possessions include the richest parts of the continent, largely because she had previously controlled most of the coast-lands.

A. The Work of the Chartered Companies

Groups of merchants gained concessions from native chiefs to open up the country for trade and settlement. They prepared the way for subsequent annexation by the home Governments which had supported them.

The most important of the British chartered companies were :

(1) *South African Company*. This was organized by Cecil Rhodes in 1889 to develop what is now called Rhodesia (see p. 114).

(2) *British East Africa Company*. A charter was granted in 1888 to work concessions in the territory belonging to the Sultan of Zanzibar. The merchants made treaties with the native chiefs of the interior in what is now called Uganda and Kenya Colony. Owing to difficulties which arose because of German rivalry, the company sought the help of the British Government, which established a protectorate over the area in 1894.

(3) *Royal Niger Company*. Trade with West Africa became important owing to the increased industrial demand for palm-oil. The Niger Company was given the right to trade in the district of the Lower Niger river and to govern the territory assigned to Britain in this area at the Conference of Berlin (1884–1885).

The company gradually extended the area under British protection and helped to rid the interior of the abominable abuses of the slave-trade. In 1900 the Government claimed direct control over this protectorate—now called Nigeria. It is the most important of Britain's tropical possessions in Africa.

B. British Expansion in Egypt and the Sudan

After the purchase of the Suez Canal Shares in 1875 Britain was committed to an interest in Egypt. The necessity of preserving order led to a military occupation.

In 1898 the Sudan was reconquered, and Kitchener forced the French to leave Fashoda. This gave Britain a practical control over all the Nile valley and brought nearer to fulfilment Rhodes's dream of an all-British route from the Cape to Cairo.

MAP 33

SOUTH AFRICA

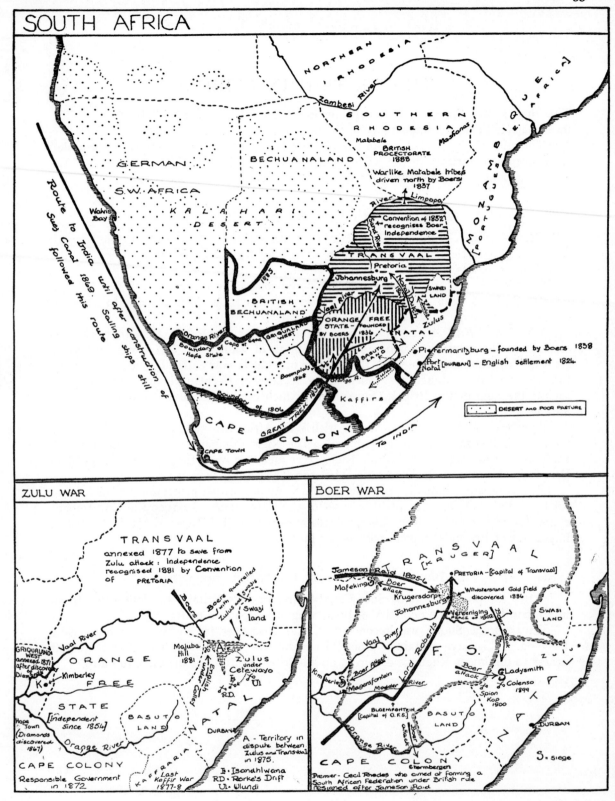

NORTHERN RHODESIA

Zambesi River

SOUTHERN RHODESIA

Matabele   Mashonas

BRITISH PROTECTORATE 1888

Warlike Matabele tribes driven north by Boers 1837

Route to India until after construction of Suez Canal 1869. Sailing ships still followed this route

GERMAN S.W. AFRICA

Walvis Bay

KALAHARI DESERT

BECHUANALAND

River Limpopo

Convention of 1852 recognises Boer Independence

TRANSVAAL

Pretoria

Johannesburg

BRITISH BECHUANALAND

SWAZI LAND

Zulus

ORANGE FREE STATE - FOUNDED BY BOERS 1836

Orange River Boundary of Cape of Good Hope State

GRIQUALAND WEST

BASUTO LAND

NATAL

Pietermaritzburg - founded by Boers 1838

Port [DURBAN] - English settlement 1824

Natal

Boomplats 1848

Boundary of 1806

GREAT TREK 1836

Orange R.

Kaffirs

CAPE COLONY

CAPE TOWN

To INDIA

DESERT and POOR PASTURE

ZULU WAR

TRANSVAAL

annexed 1877 to save from Zulu attack : Independence recognised 1881 by Convention of PRETORIA

Boers quarrelled with Zulus and Swazis

Swazi land

Boers

Vaal River

GRIQUALAND WEST annexed 1871 after discovery of Diamonds

Kimberley

ORANGE FREE STATE

[Independent since 1854]

Majuba Hill 1881

English under Colley

Zulus under Cetewayo

I

R.D.

Ul

Hope Town (Diamonds discovered 1867)

Orange River

BASUTO LAND

NATAL

DURBAN

KAFFRARIA

Last Kaffir War 1877-8

CAPE COLONY

Responsible Government in 1872

A - Territory in dispute between Zulus and Transvaal in 1875.

I - Isandhlwana
RD - Rorke's Drift
Ul - Ulundi

BOER WAR

TRANSVAAL [KRUGER]

Jameson Raid 1895-6

Mafeking

Boer attack

PRETORIA - [Capital of Transvaal]

Krugersdorp

Johannesburg

Witwatersrand Gold Field discovered 1886

SWAZI LAND

Vereeniging PEACE of 1902

Boer attack

Vaal River

O. F. S.

Boer attack

Ladysmith

Colenso 1899

Spion Kop 1900

Kimberley

Boer attack

Magersfontein

Modder River

Lord Roberts

Zulus

NATAL

BLOEMFONTEIN [Capital of O.F.S.]

BASUTO LAND

DURBAN

Orange River

Boer attack

S. = siege

CAPE COLONY

Stormbergen

Premier - Cecil Rhodes who aimed at forming a South African Federation under British rule resigned after Jameson Raid

SOUTH AFRICA

CAPE COLONY, at the southern tip of Africa, was climatically the most suitable part of the continent for white settlement. Dutch settlers had migrated there since the seventeenth century. They were all farmers and used the native tribes for the heavy work. Slave-labour had made them relatively prosperous.

The colony was first occupied by Great Britain during the wars of the French Revolution, and it was purchased from the Dutch Government in 1814 because of its value as a naval station on the route to the East. After 1815, however, distress at home led to the emigration of British settlers. This brought new problems to the home Government.

(1) The Boers and British had different views about the treatment of the natives. The Boers had always owned native slaves. They particularly resented the demand of British missionaries for equality for black and white men.

(2) In the north of the colony lived free natives, usually called Kaffirs ; they were vigorous and warlike tribes who endangered the safety of the colony by constant attacks.

A. THE GREAT TREK

In 1836 the Boers left the Cape in scattered groups and crossed the frontier beyond to find new homes free from the interference of the British Government. The map shows where they went—*i.e.*, to Natal, the Orange Free State, and the Transvaal.

(1) *Causes of the Great Trek*

(a) The Dutch hated the British methods of government. They felt humiliated when the natives were given greater rights of citizenship.

(b) The Act of 1833 abolishing slavery angered the Dutch (i) because it interfered with their rights as slave-owners, and they foresaw an end of agricultural prosperity, and (ii) because they were impoverished through inadequate compensation.

(c) The Boers disapproved of the home Government's policy towards the Kaffirs, who had attacked and laid waste the country in 1834. The Governor of the colony, with the approval of the Boers, had annexed Kaffir territory, but he was forced to cancel the annexation. The Boers felt that the British Government had no regard for their safety.

(2) *Results of the Great Trek*

(a) A heritage of bitterness divided the two races.

(b) The Boers were unable to defend themselves from the native tribes in the interior. The British were therefore compelled, for their own safety, to annex new territories, *e.g.*, Natal—the home of the Zulus—in 1843.

The British Government was not anxious to shoulder new responsibilities, and the independence of the Boer States was recognized (1852–1854). For twenty years few changes occurred.

H

B. Growing Friction between the Boers and the British (1860–1890)

(1) The chief of the Basuto tribes appealed for protection against the encroachment of the Orange Free State. The British set up a protectorate over Basutoland ; this angered the Boers of the Free State.

(2) Diamonds had been discovered in the neighbourhood of Kimberley. The Griqua chief sought help of the British Government, which annexed Griqualand West in 1871. This extension of Cape Colony across the Orange River checked the expansion of the Boers westward.

(3) *The annexation of the Transvaal* (1877). This Boer state was ill-governed and bankrupt. Its aggressive attacks on the Zulus disturbed the natives elsewhere. The Boers were too weak to hold back the warlike Zulu king, Cetewayo, and to save the Transvaal the home Government under Disraeli decided to annex the colony, promising the Boers self-government.

(4) *Conquest of Zululand* (1879) ; *annexation* (1884). Fearing the loss of his independence, Cetewayo attacked the Transvaal. The Zulu army was crushed at Ulundi in 1879.

(5) *Boer rising in the Transvaal* (1881). The British defeat at Isandhlwana in the Zulu War (1879) had lowered their prestige in the eyes of the Boers. When the Zulu War was over and there was no longer any danger of Zulu attacks, the Boers demanded their independence. Though Gladstone supported their claim, he delayed the grant of self-government, and the Boers took up arms, defeating the British at Majuba Hill in 1881. Undeterred by the military disaster, Gladstone, sympathetic to the claims of the Boers, granted their demands.

(6) *Cecil Rhodes*. The wealthy chairman of the Kimberley diamond-mines, Prime Minister of the Cape (1890–1896), was inspired by a belief in the mission of Great Britain to extend a civilizing influence throughout the world. His self-imposed task was to extend British influence in South Africa. He dreamed of a united Africa under British rule, extending northward from the Cape, and he planned the construction of a Cape-to-Cairo railway through British territory.

(a) He used his influence with the home Government to secure a protectorate over Bechuanaland (1884), fearing that the Germans in South-west Africa would intervene and thus block British expansion northward.

(b) Bechuanaland was a 'key position' in South Africa, as it lay on the direct route to the rich Zambesi valley, which it was Rhodes's ambition to control. He established the British South Africa Company in 1889, and was granted the right by charter to develop the resources of the country now bearing his name—Rhodesia.

(c) His ambitions brought him into conflict with the Boers. Their leader, Paul Kruger, deeply resented a policy of expansion which led to the encircling of Boer territory.

C. Events leading to the Boer War

(1) *Discovery of gold in the Witwatersrand* (1886). The Boers were farmers, and the gold-mines were largely run by British settlers. The rapid development of the mines led to a great increase in the number of the British—' Uitlanders '—who soon outnumbered the Boer population of the Transvaal.

Kruger adopted a policy of hostility towards them. They were denied all political rights and were heavily taxed. Moreover, monopolies granted to Europeans and heavy railway rates hampered the mining-industry.

(2) *The Jameson Raid* (1896). Dr Jameson, administrator of Rhodesia, supported by Cecil Rhodes, engineered a plot of the Uitlanders to overthrow the Boer Government of the Transvaal. The expedition was a failure; it led to the fall of Rhodes, discredited the British Government in the eyes of the world, and united both Boer states against Britain.

(3) *The Uitlanders' petition.* The Uitlanders of the Transvaal continued to agitate for improved conditions, and petitioned the British Government to intervene on their behalf. Negotiations failed to effect a compromise, owing to the obstinacy of Kruger and the uncompromising imperialism of the home Government (Chamberlain).

The Boers declared war in 1899.

D. THE BOER WAR (1899–1902)

Kruger underestimated the strength of Britain. He expected German support.

(1) The British had few troops in South Africa, and the Boers were able to invade the British territory to the east, west, and south. They besieged Mafeking, Kimberley, and Ladysmith.

(2) In 1899 large reinforcements were sent under the command of Roberts and Kitchener. The Boers were defeated, and the besieged towns relieved. Lord Roberts entered Johannesburg and Pretoria, the capital of the Transvaal. (It was annexed in 1900.)

(3) The Boers refused to submit and for two years carried on an irregular warfare from their scattered farms and homesteads. Kitchener finally wore down their resistance, and peace was signed at Vereeniging in 1902.

The Boer republics were annexed, but the Boers were promised the right to govern themselves. They were compensated for war damage to their farms.

E. UNION OF SOUTH AFRICA (1909)

The union included the two British colonies, Cape of Good Hope (which had secured responsible government in 1872) and Natal (which had been self-governing since 1893), and the two former Boer republics, Transvaal and the Orange River Colony (to which a similar privilege was extended in 1907).

There were difficult problems to settle in South Africa, and it was essential that a common policy should be adopted in all the states—*e.g.*, attitude towards the natives, customs, and railways. To settle these problems satisfactorily, a constitution was drafted which was accepted by the British Parliament in 1909.

MAP 34

IMPERIAL PROBLEMS

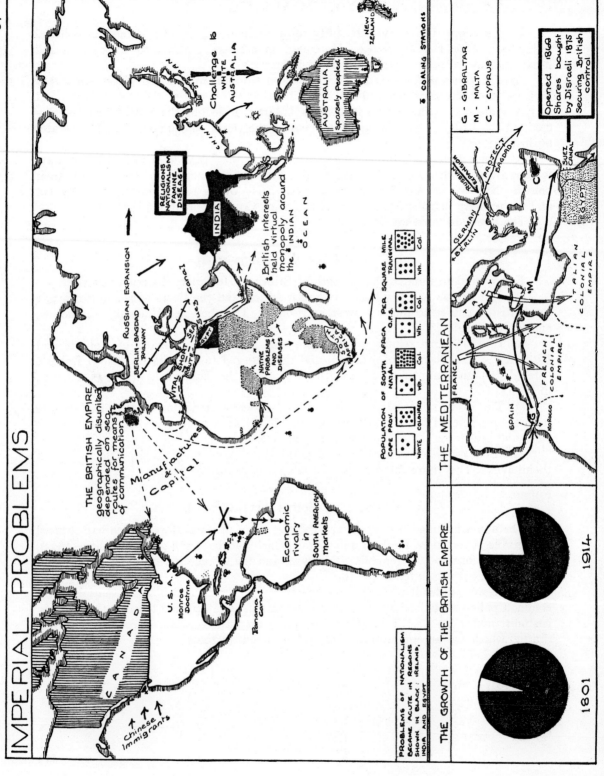

THE BRITISH EMPIRE geographically disunited depended on sea routes for means of communication

Chinese Immigrants

CANADA

U.S.A.
Monroe Doctrine

Panama Canal

Economic rivalry in South American markets

Manufactures & Capital

RUSSIAN EXPANSION

BERLIN-BAGDAD RAILWAY

VITAL SHORT ROUTE — Suez Canal

SEA ROUTE

Suez Canal

SOUTH AFRICA

Native Problems and Diseases

INDIA

RELIGIONS NATIONALISM FAMINE DISEASE

·British interests held virtual monopoly around the INDIAN OCEAN

CHINA

Challenge to WHITE AUSTRALIA

AUSTRALIA Sparsely peopled

NEW ZEALAND

PROBLEMS OF NATIONALISM BECAME ACUTE IN REGIONS SHOWN IN BLACK: IRELAND, INDIA AND EGYPT

POPULATION OF SOUTH AFRICA PER SQUARE MILE

CAPE PROV.	NATAL	O.F.S.	TRANSVAAL
WHITE COLOURED	Wh. Col.	Wh. Col.	Wh. Col.

☆ COALING STATIONS

THE GROWTH OF THE BRITISH EMPIRE

1801

1914

THE MEDITERRANEAN

RUSSIAN EXPANSION

GERMAN BERLIN

PROJECT BAGDAD»

FRANCE

SPAIN

MOROCCO

ITALY

'M'

FRENCH COLONIAL EMPIRE

ITALIAN COLONIAL EMPIRE

'G'

SUEZ CANAL

EGYPT

'C'

G - GIBRALTAR
M - MALTA
C - CYPRUS

Opened 1869 Shares bought by Disraeli 1875 securing British control

IMPERIAL PROBLEMS

THE great and rapid expansion of the Empire during the nineteenth century increased the responsibilities of British statesmen. The territories under the British flag became so varied and widespread—including about one quarter of the area and population of the globe—that racial, religious, or economic troubles can take place hardly anywhere in the world without somehow affecting the political or financial interests of Britain.

The major problems concern :
(a) The securing of unity within the Empire.
(b) The growth of nationalism.
(c) International rivalry.
(d) The economic development of the Empire.

A. THE PROBLEM OF SECURING UNITY WITHIN THE EMPIRE

Until the last few decades of the century the attitude of British statesmen towards the colonies had been mainly one of indifference. Disraeli had done much to arouse interest and pride in the Empire, but had put forward no constructive schemes for confederation. This was the work of Joseph Chamberlain. He proposed new political and economic ties to bind the Empire more closely together.

(1) *The Imperial Conferences.* The Queen's Jubilee in 1887 had brought together representatives from all the colonies. Chamberlain developed the accidental meeting of colonial premiers into a permanent institution—the Imperial Conference. Out of this conference developed the Committee for Imperial Defence, a body which made a systematic study of the problems connected with the adequate defence of the Empire.

(2) *Imperial preference.* As Colonial Minister (1895–1902) Chamberlain proposed that the Empire should be bound together by a tariff system. His suggestion of taxing imports, giving a lower preferential duty on colonial goods, was rejected by the British people in the election of 1906.

B. NATIONALISM

(1) *Ireland,* the closest of Britain's possessions, was spiritually remote—the least sympathetic to the imperial idea. Its demand for Home Rule (and, later, complete independence) was difficult to grant, because :
(a) Its close proximity made it a strategical necessity of the defences of Britain. Its coasts might furnish innumerable bases for a submarine blockade of England.
(b) Protestant Ulster, as patriotic as Catholic south was disloyal, was opposed to separation.

(2) *South Africa.* There were three racial problems in the Union of South Africa :
(a) *Boers v. British.* Disputes arose between those states of the union which were predominantly of British settlement and those in which the Boers were in the majority concerning differences in language, customs duties, the treatment of the natives, and immigration from India.
(b) *White v. black.* The natives outnumbered the whites by four and a half to one. Any attempt by British statesmen to improve their education or status was resented by the Boers (*cp.* the Rand miners' strike, 1913).
(c) *Immigrants from India.* Asiatic natives were brought over about 1880 to work in the sugar-plantations of Natal. Like the blacks, they have a low standard of life and they tend to displace the ' poor whites.' (*N.B.* Any harsh treatment of Hindus causes complaints from India ; there is no powerful African community to object to the exploitation of the black people.)

In Rhodesia there was trouble owing to the displacement of the natives from their lands and the restrictions placed on their movement. The provision of ' native reservations ' had avoided this difficulty in Nigeria, Canada, and New Zealand.

(3) *Egypt.* The nationalist movement began the moment England occupied the country in 1881. The problem of granting independence was complicated by :
(a) The defence of the Suez Canal.
(b) Financial indebtedness ; the Egyptians had borrowed large sums of money from British financiers.
(c) The Sudan ; turbulent Arab tribes continued to disturb the protectorate, and the removal of British troops would have made the defence of the Sudan impossible.

(4) *India.* Britain's main aim was to develop trade with India, her best customer ; but this involved the government of 300,000,000 people of diverse languages, races, and religions.

Unruly tribes on the frontiers, religious (Moslem *v.* Hindu) disorders in the cities, divided control in the native states, economic problems (poverty, disease, and famine), and the fear of Russian aggression caused problems of the first magnitude.

C. International Rivalry

After 1870 Britain had to face the problem of foreign competition (see p. 86).

The Empire is spread out over the seven seas ; its most striking geographical characteristic is its disunity. It is knit together by oceans, and its control depends on sea-power.

(1) *Germany.* German attempts to complete the Berlin-Bagdad railway would have short-circuited the Mediterranean-Suez route to the East.

(2) *Russia.* The extension of Russian dominion towards Afghanistan and Persia threatened the land-communications to India.

(3) *France.* The French encroached eastward along the Sudan grasslands and reached the Nile at Fashoda. This expansion threatened the all-British Cape-to-Cairo route.

France also developed the south-eastern part of Asia in Indo-China, inconveniently near to Malaya and Singapore.

(4) *Japan.* The Westernization of Japan and its need for increased territory threatened the empty Australian continent. The maintenance of a 'white Australia' became an increasingly difficult problem.

N.B. These major problems occur in countries round the Indian Ocean. The map shows how most of the land round this ocean is under the British flag.

D. ECONOMIC DEVELOPMENT

These problems have been dealt with on pp. 85–86.

EXERCISES

(1)

    (i) Areas A are the most densely populated regions of Great Britain to-day. Give reasons.

    (ii) When was area B the most populated part of Britain? Why? Account for the change.

    (iii) Identify towns C, D, and E. Arrange them in order of size and importance in the eighteenth, nineteenth, and twentieth centuries. What trade made these ports prosperous?

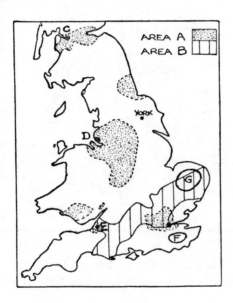

    (iv) What industries were carried on in areas F and G in the eighteenth century? Give reasons for their decay.

    (v) How long did a journey from London to York take in 1700, in 1800, and in 1850? Give reasons for your answers.

(2) On an outline-map of Northern England insert name and date:

    (i) A road repaired by John Metcalf.

    (ii) A bridge built by Thomas Telford.

    (iii) A canal constructed by James Brindley.

    (iv) A railway built by George Stephenson.

(3)
    (i) Give three reasons for the historical importance of the food-crop shown by dots.
    (ii) What movement is suggested by the arrows B ? When did it take place, and why ?
    (iii) What movement is suggested by the arrows C ? What political society developed later as a result of this emigration ?
    (iv) When, and by whom, were trade unions developed in area D ? What were the difficulties of union organization in this area ?

(4) On an outline-map of Southern England insert :
    (i) The route of the Bath stage-coach from London. How long did this journey take in 1784 ?
    (ii) The route of the West Indies mail. Mark and name the port.
    (iii) The first broad-gauge line built by Brunel. Mark a town which was created by this railway.

    Insert the following places, and state briefly what important event is associated with each of them :

        The Nore, Spithead, Grampound, Speenhamland, Tolpuddle, Newport (Mon.).

(5) On an outline-map of England :
    (i) Shade in distinctive colours the areas in which (a) population grew rapidly after the Industrial Revolution, (b) the Luddite Riots took place, and (c) six counties which were over-represented in the 1830 Parliament.
    (ii) Mark and date (d) the route of the Blanketeers' march, (e) Spa Fields, (f) Kennington Common, (g) Taff Vale, and (h) Peterloo fields. Of what historical significance are these places ?

(6)

    (i) Identify river A, ports B and C, forts D and E, and battles F, G, H, and J.
    (ii) Who took route K ?   Why was this campaign unsuccessful ?
    (iii) Describe Wellington's campaign along route L, and correlate with Napoleon's
        campaigns in the rest of Europe.

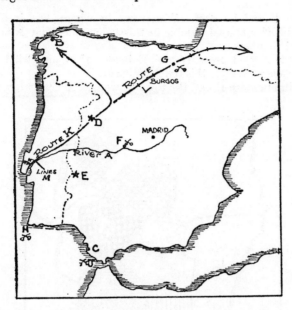

    (iv) What city was defended by lines M ?   Why did the French lift their siege ?
    (v) When did Wellington attempt the capture of forts D and E ?   Give two reasons
        why their fall would have been important.

(7)

    (i) On either an outline-map of Western Europe or by means of a diagram explain
        the purpose of the Battle of Trafalgar.
    (ii) Use red and blue crayons to show (a) by continuous lines, the routes taken by
        the British and enemy fleets, and (b) by dotted lines, the routes the enemy
        proposed to follow.

(8)

    Draw sketch-maps to illustrate the journey of a soldier who came from India to
    the Crimea, fought at Inkerman, and was invalided to the Scutari Hospital.

(9)

(i) Name river A and the man who first explored this district.

(ii) Name river C and its tributary B. In what circumstances did colony G expand across river C? What effect had this expansion on each of districts D, E, and L?

(iii) Name area F and its port. When, and by whom, was it first settled? What native peoples caused trouble in this colony? What Asiatic people live here in large numbers?

(iv) What people settled areas D and E before 1836, and what was their principal occupation? Why is this date significant?

(v) Name capital of state D and the town in which the Uitlanders lived.

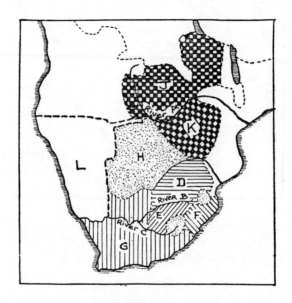

(iv) Of what status in the British Empire are the areas shown with dots? What was the special importance of area H about 1885, and why was it annexed?

(vii) Name area L and the European power which annexed it. Account for the sparse population of this region.

(viii) Name areas J and K. In area J there are only five people per square mile, and of these less than one in a hundred is white. Give reasons for this.

(ix) What are the principal obstacles to successful farming in areas J and K? By what means were they opened up to British traders?

(x) When and why did the British Parliament legislate for the Union of areas D, E, F, and G?

(10)

(i) Identify island Y, and explain how it got its name.

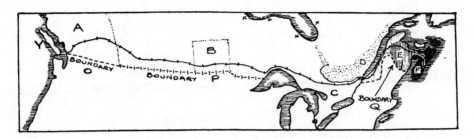

(ii) Name the trans-continental railway, and state (*a*) one political reason for its construction, (*b*) the date of its completion, and (*c*) the economic effect of its construction on colony B.

(iii) When did provinces A, B, E, and F join the Dominion?

(iv) By what treaties were the boundaries O, P, and Q settled?

(v) Of what significance were the places round Hudson's Bay that are marked with crosses?

(vi) In what ways do the people of C differ from those in D?

(11) On an outline-map of Africa insert and name:

(i) The four great rivers. Then insert the following names where you think they are most appropriate, giving reasons for your decision: Speke, Mungo Park, Stanley, Rhodes, Lugard, Livingstone.

(ii) An area in which the exploitation of the natives caused a great outcry in Europe.

(iii) Two areas to which natives of India were attracted.

(iv) An area which became important with the invention of margarine in 1870.

(v) The states which remained independent in 1914.

(12) On an outline-map of British North America insert and name:

(i) The four provinces which formed the Dominion in 1867.

(ii) The colony which has never joined the Dominion.

(iii) The area in which gold-mining became important in 1897.

(iv) The boundary which was not settled until 1902.

Shade and name the areas which developed rapidly only after the building of railways.

(13)

(i) Name navigators O and P. When did they make the voyages shown? Identify X, where navigator P landed. Of what significance was this landing?

(ii) Identify colony A. What was its original name? Why was it the last of the Australian colonies to receive responsible government?

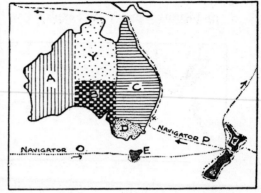

(iii) In what respects did the original settlement of colony B differ from that of D or E?

(iv) Name colony C. Between what dates did it have the boundaries shown? When was the northern part separated, and what colony did it become? What important event occurred in this decade which affected the political status of these colonies?

(v) Account for the straightness of the frontier-lines and the irregularity of the boundary between colonies C and D.

(vi) Give the present and former names of island E. Why was the name changed?

(vii) Give reasons to explain the sparse population of (*a*) the northern part and (*b*) the southern part of area Y.

(viii) For what purpose were islands F and G first used by Europeans? What native peoples lived there? In which of the two islands were they more numerous?

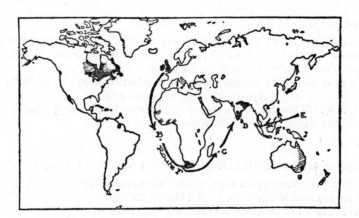

(14)

(i) At what date did the British Empire comprise only the areas shown?

(ii) Identify islands A, B, C, D, and E.

(iii) When did they become part of the Empire, and in what circumstances were they acquired?

(iv) About what time did route F cease to be the most important way to India? Give reasons.

INDEX

BATTLES, SIEGES

TREATIES, CONGRESSES